Tales o' the Maisters

Tales o' the Maisters

A History
of
Kemnay School
1820 – 1948

by

Duncan A Downie
Donald M Morrison
Anna M Muirhead

Text Donald Morrison, Anna Muirhead
and Duncan Downie 1995 ©
Line Drawings David Duthie 1995 ©

Published by
Time Pieces Publications
Kirkstyle
KEMNAY
Aberdeenshire AB51 5PJ

All Rights Reserved. No part of this publication may be reproduced, stored in a retrieval system, or transmitted in any form or by any means, electronic, mechanical, photocopying, recording or otherwise, without the prior written permission of the copyright owner.

Typeset from author generated disc by
Reflective Images, Insch, Aberdeenshire

Printed by
BPC – AUP Aberdeen Ltd

ISBN 1 899966 00 5

Contents

Introduction	1
Andrew Stevenson	7
George Proctor	39
William Alexander	50
John Minto Robertson	55
Teachers	91
School Buildings	99
School Board Members	108
School Log Books 1873 – 1948	114
John A Morgan	144
Acknowledgements	151

Photographs and Illustrations

Kemnay Academy and Parish School	Front Cover
Sketch of Kemnay School circa 1841	7
Andrew Stevenson's Gravestone	30
Portrait of Andrew Stevenson	38
Kemnay School circa 1893	47
Advertisement for Shakespeare play 1946	57
Cast from 'A Winter's Tale'	58
Cast from 'Much Ado About Nothing'	59
Kemnay Girl Guides	62
Kemnay Boy Scouts	63
Dux Board	67
School Badge	68
Home Guard	72
Mr and Mrs John Minto Robertson	84
Kemnay Secondary School	85
1911 Class Photograph	86
1922 Class Photograph	87
Junior Infants April 1933	88
School Percussion Band 1945	89
School Report of 1933	90
Photograph of Teachers 1947	93
Map of Kemnay 1792	99
Drawing of School Building in 1874	102
Drawing of School Building in 1879	102
Drawing of School Building in 1894	104
Plan of School Buildings 1860 – 1994	106
Photograph of Kemnay School in 1905	107
Presentation of School Prizes	132

Introduction

On his arrival at Kemnay Academy as history teacher, Donald Morrison was concerned at the lack of local history materials. A small group was formed, consisting of Donald, Anna Muirhead, the school librarian and Duncan Downie, a local researcher. Others joined in from time to time to assist the committee with their services.

It was decided to research Education in the Parish of Kemnay up to 1948, the year when the school was reduced from a Senior Secondary to a Junior Secondary School. Funds were received from the Community Education Department permitting the employment of an interviewer, who contacted a number of former pupils with a questionnaire regarding their schooldays. The results of these interviews were collated and were soon in use as a pupil resource in the school library.

As very little primary information could be found regarding the parish school of Kemnay prior to the early part of the nineteenth century, it was decided that research should be concentrated on the four headmasters covering the period from 1820 to 1948. These were Andrew Stevenson, George Proctor, William Alexander and J Minto Robertson. Andrew Stevenson proved to be well documented, which made research on George Proctor somewhat more difficult, as very little information on his work was found prior to 1873. William Alexander was remembered at first hand by the older members of the community, whereas J Minto Robertson was almost a legend in his own time, as well as a prolific writer of school logs.

The project would not have succeeded without the considerable help given by the Regional Archivist who supplied data, both in original form and by photocopy, for research as needed. These photocopies, which were funded by the Community Education Department, have been placed in the Academy library as a resource for pupil research.

Much time was spent in general research in the School Log books, School Board Minutes, and other relevant material, with no specific idea as to how the final layout would appear. Although the members of the committee became engrossed in the subject, there was always the thought as to how it would be received publicly. What the researchers found of interest might not prove to be so with the public. As the months passed, the picture that began to appear became ever more interesting. Names became characters, forgotten people reappeared. A tapestry of village life was being woven before the eyes of those involved.

The gestation period has been lengthy, and for this the committee apologises. This came about for several reasons. The fact that no deadline had been set initially, possibly allowed more in-depth research than may have been anticipated. The departure of both Anna and Donald from the Academy affected the regularity with which the committee could meet. The continuing interest of members of the public in the project finally urged on a publication date.

The committee, wish to thank all those who have helped, both knowingly and unknowingly, especially Miss Mary H Duncan and Mr Gordon R Ingram for their considerable help on the work of J Minto Robertson, and Mr David Duthie for his help with work on the school buildings. We hope that the book will be gratefully received by friends both at home and further afield.

Scottish Education – Historical Background

In order to understand the history and development of Kemnay School, a brief look at the history of education in general and the parish school in particular, is necessary.

Early Education

Education was originally run by the Church and there were mainly three types of schools :

Cathedral or monastery schools from which the burgh or grammar school developed.

the Parish school, which before and after the Reformation played an important role in Scottish education.

'song schools' or lecture schools which gave an elementary education in the burghs.

The curriculum of grammar and song schools was based on the demands of church services, for nearly all students of higher education were destined for the ministry. So pupils would be taught to read, write and speak Latin.

The highest classes would probably have been taught Logic at least until the fifteenth century when it was concentrated in the Universities.

In 1496, Scotland got its first Education Act which required the eldest sons and heirs of Barons and substantial freeholders to be sent to grammar schools at 8 or 9 to perfect Latin before going on to spend 3 years at the schools of Art and Jure so that they might have understanding of the laws.

Unfortunately, there is no evidence that this law was enforced. It seems to have stemmed from a desire on the part of James IV to build up a civil service rather than any consideration of education for itself.

The Effect of the Reformation

The years immediately before the Reformation had seen some liberal moves in education. The Act of 1543 allowed everyone to own and read (if they could) the Holy Scriptures and an Act in 1559 stated that any parish clerks who were incompetent in preaching to be put to study in the schools. In general, the challenge of the Reformers prompted the Church to improve the education it provided.

However, the Reformation proceeded and it had a strong effect on education in the long term. The Presbyterian Church which was established in 1560 held that schools were necessary to establish the Reformed faith, and a complete scheme for the reorganisation of Scottish education was drawn up – the Book of Discipline. Although this was rejected by Parliament in January 1561 and never passed into law, it is generally accepted as an important document because it outlines many of the ideas and frameworks which were later adopted and form the basis of the 'traditional' Scottish education.

It had aimed at a whole national view of education and saw education as the right of all with bursaries for the clever poor (it only mentioned boys, of course!). The Book of Discipline had also proposed small rural parish schools and a rational organisation of the universities. This is what in fact happened over the next few centuries so that for example, by the late 19th century, more poor boys got into university in Scotland than any other country in Europe.

Between the Reformation and 1696, several Acts were passed to ensure that a school was set up in every parish, but it was not until the 1696 Act of Settling Schools that the conditions and terms for each parish school were laid out. It stated that there should be a school provided and schoolmaster appointed where there was not already one in existence. The school was to be housed 'commodiously' and the teacher's salary was fixed at a minimum of 100 and maximum of 200 merks a year (£5 11s 1d to £11 2s 3d sterling).

The heritors (landholders) were to be responsible for this cost and the school itself, but they could recover half their costs from their tenants. Unlike previous Acts, there was an effort to enforce this one and heritors could be fined if they did not carry it out.

Parish Schools

The rural mainstay of Scottish education was the parish school. The school buildings varied – they might be purpose-built by a generous landowner or more probably they would be a humble or wretched hut.

By the middle of the 19th century however, the average accommodation was one or two small rooms for the master and a schoolroom.

In the Old Statistical Account (1790's), which was compiled from parish reports, many references are made to education. While this reflects the high regard in which education was held in the parishes, there is a general complaint about the availability and standard of schoolmasters.

> 'the want of proper schoolmasters is the principal cause of the ignorance, bigotry and sectarianism which now prevails in many parts of this country' (O.S.A.)

It was not the teaching profession which was blamed for this state of affairs, but rather the heritors and others who were unwilling to provide any decent funds. The message from the parish reports was clear – the profession must be made more attractive to educated men.

The 1803 Education Act sought to do this in several ways – new rates of pay were set for the dominie, fees were to be fixed by the heritors and rates hung in the schoolroom, although the dominies had to teach free any poor children of the parish. The teachers had to be provided with a school house and garden at least a quarter of a Scots acre, the house at least two rooms. New teachers had to be examined and approved by the Presbytery. The Presbytery regulated teaching hours and what teachers could be dismissed for – neglect of duty, immoral behaviour and cruel treatment of pupils. But it was the heritors who had to pay for this, so although the Church was involved in the running of the school, greater power lay with the heritors who provided the funding.

So, by 1827, over 400 out of 906 parish schools had masters who had done a four year university course and graduates were the norm in the North-East where the Dick Bequest inspector set high standards.

But there were still problems in the period up to 1872 – in most rural areas, children went to school at 4 or 5 or even 6 if they lived further out from the schoolhouse. In general, five years education was the norm. But seasonal considerations meant that no real start would be made in schools until Martinmas (28th November) and attendance was generally good until

March–April when agricultural influences kept children away.

Apart from the difficulties which arose from these patterns of attendance, there was some obstruction from parents who objected to the teaching of Latin or even arithmetic.

The teacher also had to cope with perhaps 100 pupils ranging from 5 to 13 in a small cramped room. Despite the Act of 1803, standards of accommodation varied greatly and often the schoolmaster himself would improve and extend the allocated building (such was the case at Kemnay under the influence of Andrew Stevenson).

In 1867, the Argyll Commission investigated the funding of parish schools. Their recommendations were incorporated into the 1872 Education Act which allowed for the levying of an educational rate. It was from here on that the state accepted its responsibilities for educating the new industrial society and this Act marks the beginning of the end for the parish school. For although the Act safeguarded the Secondary work done in parish schools, it set up the Scottish Education Department and elected school boards to take over the powers formally held by heritors and the Church. Education at home or at school became compulsory between 5–13. This was earlier than in England where it was not so until Acts in 1881 and 1891.

In 1888, the Leaving Certificate was introduced. This was to be a spur to the development of separate elementary and secondary education. Originally offered at three levels, it could be taken in any subject at any time. In 1908, a group leaving certificate was introduced which required passes at one sitting in either four Highers or three Highers and two Lowers. This lasted until the 1950's when group requirements were abolished in favour of individual subject passes.

In 1918, local County and City Education Authorities were set up and throughout the 1920's and 1930's, more and more of these educational authorities adopted the 'clean cut' approach by which children were transferred to some kind of post-primary education at about 12. Many parish schools continued but generally, with the raising of the school leaving age, the move was towards separate schools.

Andrew Stevenson

Of all the men who have held the post of headmaster at Kemnay School, one of the most colourful and well documented is Andrew Stevenson. Born in 1794 in humble circumstances in the parish of Chapel of Garioch, which nestles round the eastern slopes of Bennachie, he received little or no formal education.

The parish minister of Kemnay, Rev. Dr. Patrick Mitchell, took the lad under his wing and had him ready for entry to Aberdeen University when the parish school became vacant through the death of Charles Dawson in July 1820. His name was put forward and Andrew Stevenson became master of Kemnay Parish School.

Parish schools of these days were far from luxurious. More often they were two roomed hovels, the master staying in one, the other being the schoolroom. It was not long before he set about improving the property and by 1823 we find him requesting a piece of ground from the laird to build a house for his ageing father on the understanding that when he dies, the house will become the property of the laird. (Burnett Papers, Bundle 44) Fifteen years elapse before Stevenson gets another mention in the Kemnay estate papers. Here, he is again petitioning for building materials, but this time it is for getting the thatch of the school repaired. When he had been given permission to have the roof done, Stevenson asked the estate worker to put in new thatch as well, but 'John would not give any without (Burnett's) orders so that it is not done'. The factor went on to say that: 'I was looking at it. I think it is not in great want of it but as it was only a very small quantity that was wanted, I suppose it would be as weal to get it done'. (Kemnay House papers 17.1.1838) Stevenson's subsequent concern for maintaining and improving the fabric of the school led to its transformation from a thatched, 'smoky hut' to the elegant establishment represented in the sketch below.

Stevenson went on to build up the school, both in terms of its structure and its reputation as an educational institution of merit. At his own expense, he added to the school buildings and even set up his own boarding school for 'boys of a higher class'. (New Statistical Account p820) He was one of only nine schoolmasters in the north-east of Scotland to take in private boarders as an adjunct to the parish school.

The 1841 census for Kemnay makes many references to education. Among the remarks by George Peter, the local minister we find:
"The increase in population since 1831 is accounted for ...by the flourishing condition of an Academy conducted by Mr Stevenson".

It is also noted that the four enumerators who conducted the census were all boarding pupils of Mr Stevenson.

However in spite of, or maybe because of all the success and acclamation bestowed on Mr Stevenson, he also had his detractors – most notably a Mr Menzies, the inspector of schools for the Dick Bequest. Although impressed by the outward appearance of the school, Menzies was not so taken with Stevenson's teaching ability. When the latter refused to take advice about how to improve the school, he had his Dick Bequest allowance withdrawn. There then proceeded a bitter war of words between the Trustees of the Dick Bequest and a committee of Garioch Presbytery who strongly supported Stevenson against the 'incompetence' of the Trustees. This dragged on for several years, culminating in the publication on both sides of detailed submissions of their complaints against each other.

By this time (1852–3), the arguments had become so entrenched that there was no hope for a compromise solution, especially since the Aberdeen Journal was providing its readers with a blow by blow account and at the same time fanning the controversy. The local paper incidentally sided with Stevenson, the north-east man struggling against the tyranny of an Edinburgh bureaucracy. What follows is a detailed account of the case of Andrew Stevenson and his Kemnay Academy – a case which was ultimately to be taken to the very highest court of appeal, the House of Lords.

To gain an insight into how Stevenson's circumstances aroused such public interest, we need to know a little about the origins of the Dick Bequest and its influence on the educational system in the north-east at this time. James Dick was born in Forres, but spent most of his life outside Scotland. At the age of nineteen, he went out to Jamaica where he made his money working in a mercantile house. He came back and settled in London for the duration of his life. There, he added to his wealth by 'judicious speculation'. He died on May 24th 1828, aged 83. In his will, he bequeathed nearly all of his estate to the benefit of teachers in the north-east of Scotland. The Bequest came into operation in 1832 and amounted to a colossal £113,147. The capital generated an annual interest of £3,597 which was to be used to supplement teachers' meagre earnings.

1841 Census Kemnay   **Schoolhouse 8th June 1841**

Name	Age	Occupation	Where born
Andrew Stevenson	45	Schoolmaster	S
Andrew Farquhar	12	Scholar	S
George Thomson	15	"	I
Alexr Walker	10	"	S
James Whyte	9	"	S
John Farquhar	10	"	I
Alexr Emslie	15	"	S
Francis Brown	13	"	S
James Stephen	13	"	S
John Simpson	12	"	S
James Gray	13	"	S
Gordon Watt	14	"	I
James Abel	9	"	S
James Houston	13	"	I
Leslie Clark	9	"	S
Alexr Lindsay	15	"	S
Peter Hay	12	"	S
Strachan Massie	14	"	E
John Ogilvy	9	"	S
John Lunan	10	"	S
George Ferguson	14	"	S
William Walker	7	"	S
Isabel Angus	20	Female Servant	S
Jane Gordon	15	"	S

S – Scotland; E – England; I – Ireland

Dick's original intention was to have the Bequest administered by the Principals and Professors of Kings and Marischal Colleges at Aberdeen. However, for some reason, he changed his mind and decided to appoint another Board of Trustees. Unfortunately, he died before his detailed instructions for the regulation of the fund could be signed. The new Trustees had to be appointed by the Court of Chancery which comprised 11 members of the Society of Writers to the Signet. They took office in June 1829. When the Bequest started in 1832, there were 137 parochial schools eligible for grants. The Royal Burghs of Banff, Elgin and Forres were to be excluded because their schools were not parochial – 'their appointments flowing exclusively from the magistrates and town councils of the respective burghs'. Kintore was made an exception to the rule because its schoolmasters were parochial 'in every sense of the term'.

Assistance from the Bequest was only available for teachers over the age of 21. The Trustees found that in the north-east, not all schoolmasters were University educated – in fact, 'many headmasters were appointed at the ages of eighteen or nineteen, and in one or two instances so early as fifteen and sixteen'. Under the rules of the Bequest, every teacher, whether a University graduate or not, had to pass a gruelling examination in literature and science. This entrance requirement into the Bequest was started in 1835, but did not apply to those who had been receiving a grant from the Bequest before 1835. This included Stevenson who was an original participant. The exam was held in Edinburgh over a two day period and lasted 15 hours in total. On top of that, teachers were assessed on their practical teaching abilities.

In the early years of the Bequest, allowances were kept in line with the schoolmasters' other earnings, so that those who earned more got a larger Dick allowance. From 1843 onwards though, the Trustees decided that teachers should get paid according to other, more discernible criteria such as the quality of the teaching, the regularity of attendance of the pupils and the amount of the school fees. For these to be judged fairly, schools would have to be inspected on a regular basis.

Although they took into account reports sent in by local committees representing the 13 Presbyteries covering the north-east, the Trustees decided to appoint their own Visitor to inspect schools and hopefully to elevate educational standards. At this time, the Trustees considered teachers and clergy to be 'prejudiced against educational innovations', so that they would have to use the granting of allowances as both carrot and stick to bring about the improvements they desired.

Teachers were quite poorly paid in those days, the average income being £55 12s 4d. If we add an average allowance of £25 10s 3d from the Dick Bequest, we can say that parochial schoolmasters in the mid-1830s in the north-east of Scotland earned about £81 a year. Clearly, the extra allowance from the Bequest was a very important addition to schoolmasters' income, and so, one can imagine that there would be a certain amount of anxiety in the various parish schools at the time of the Dick Bequest inspector's visit. We know, from the New Statistical Account of Scotland that Stevenson's salary in 1842 was only £25 13s 4d, supplemented by 'the interest of 850 merks Scots, bequeathed, many years ago, by different individuals, for promoting education in the parish'. (New Statistical Account p820)

According to his last will and testament (18.5.1827) Dick's intention was to give financial support to 'that neglected, though useful class of men, and to add to their very trifling salaries'. As to the role of the Trustees, he laid out several guidelines:

They were to have full power to decide which of the school-masters would benefit from the fund; also how much they should get.

They should use the fund to 'encourage active schoolmasters, and gradually to elevate the literary character of the Parochial Schoolmasters and schools

To this purpose, the Trustees could increase, decrease or discontinue the allowance of any or all the schoolmasters without being accountable for doing so.

The Trustees were to pay particular attention to the qualifications and diligence of the schoolmasters, particularly in their preparation of students for College and their supervision during the intervals between terms. However, this should not be done at the expense of the 'common branches of education' in the parish school.

The Trustees were authorised to appoint a properly qualified person to act as their Clerk. They also had the power to hire and fire the Clerk for whatever reason and to decide on an appropriate salary for him.

Doubts about Stevenson's merits first arose after a visit to the School of Kemnay on the 8th of July 1842 by Mr Menzies, the Clerk of the Dick Bequest Trust i.e. their school inspector. Being dissatisfied with what he saw on that occasion, Menzies took the unusual step of asking Richard Mackenzie, the Deputy-Keeper of the Signet, to accompany him on a second inspection of the school ten days later. Just how impartial Mackenzie was going to be after having been given Menzies side of the story on his return to Edinburgh is anybody's guess, but it would have taken a very strong-willed person to have formed a radically different view. After all, these two gentlemen knew each other well and were of a similar mind about what made a good school. Clearly Kemnay, and Stevenson in particular, did not have what it took. Before leaving the parish, the two made a point of visiting the parish minister, the Rev. George Peter to inform him of their opinion that the teaching at the school was 'not altogether satisfactory'. (Communication to the Presbyteries within the Counties of Aberdeen, Banff, and Moray by the Trustees of the Dick Bequest, regarding the Case of Kemnay p13)

A month later, Menzies wrote to Stevenson, informing him about his concerns and suggested that he should employ a qualified assistant. According to Menzies version of events, the Rev. Peter did not object to this recommendation. Stevenson duly complied with the Dick Bequest Trust conditions and hired an assistant teacher who had had the benefit of a 'classical education', thus confirming that it was Stevenson's weakness in the classics that Menzies really wished to have rectified. Unfortunately, academic qualifications do not guarantee excellence as a teacher – such qualities as dedication, hard work, rapport with children and the ability to enthuse and motivate do not come automatically along with the university parchment. Stevenson's unnamed assistant turned out to be 'of lazy habits' and not sufficiently interested in the school – he was dismissed six months later.

As far as the Dick Bequest Trustees were concerned, Stevenson had accepted their point about his own weaknesses as a teacher and the need to rectify these by the appointment of a qualified assistant. The fact that Stevenson had objected to the individual taken on did not invalidate the principle of the need for such an assistant. However, when another six months passed and Stevenson still had not taken the necessary step, Menzies wrote again (13.9.1843) to urge him to appoint someone else. Nothing happened. For whatever reason, Stevenson was not going to be bullied or cajoled into a course of action he felt was unnecessary. When he had made no appointment by Martinmas, the Trustees decided to withhold his allowance which was now due.

The Trustees were about to make a very weak and, as it turned out, a very damaging decision which would have repercussions for the Kemnay debacle for much of the next decade. In a minute dated 14th December 1843, they reiterated their view that Stevenson should appoint a qualified assistant and that the character and success of Kemnay school depended on this. Consequently the Clerk, Mr Menzies was instructed to continue to urge Stevenson to comply with the recommendation. They also decided that:

> 'In the meantime the Treasurer was authorised to remit Mr Stevenson's allowance, the meeting being persuaded that his own right views will stimulate him to the adoption of what is so directly calculated to improve his seminary'. (Dick Bequest Trust minute 1844 – Scottish Records Office ref. GD 1/4/3)

In effect, the Trustees had, in the space of two months, sent Stevenson two conflicting messages. In the first, he had been 'punished' for his non-compliance with the Dick Bequest Trust by having his allowance withheld; now, he was to be 'rewarded' by getting his allowance reinstated even though he still had not complied with their conditions. As any teacher will testify, you should never reward bad behaviour – you are only storing up trouble for the future. The Trustees were surely being rather naive if they expected Stevenson to agree to their conditions after he had received his back-dated allowance.

As it turned out, they had badly miscalculated – Stevenson was not the sort of compliant and 'reasonable' country schoolmaster that they perhaps normally had dealings with. On the contrary, it soon became clear that Stevenson had 'taken umbrage at the interference of the Trustees'. Under the terms of Dick's will, the Trustees could increase, decrease or sever an allowance without having to give reasons. Armed with these powers, they were certainly within their rights to discontinue Stevenson's allowance until such time that they were satisfied with his behaviour. Now though, the Trustees made matters worse by deciding not to insist on Stevenson complying with their specific request to hire a qualified assistant! Instead, they seem to have been swayed by a subsequent letter written by Stevenson wherein he laid out his own proposals for improving the school, none of which involved taking on more staff.

On the 27th February 1844, the Clerk wrote to Kemnay asking Stevenson to provide evidence of all the improvements he had now adopted. One of the key measures proposed was to send his assistant to Edinburgh to improve his teaching techniques. This was never done, although Stevenson himself did attend the Circus Place School in Edinburgh in November 1844 to observe what the Trustees considered to be 'improved methods of instruction'. The Trustees' own minutes reveal that Stevenson was not considered to be in most need of improvement – whereas he was only 'recommended' to visit the model school, the schoolmasters of Auchindoir and Drumblade were 'required' to attend. (Dick Bequest Trust minutes 1844 – SRO ref. GD 1/4/3)

From a reading of the Dick Bequest Trust's version of events, they were at pains to bend over backwards to accommodate Stevenson. In doing so, they had undoubtedly muddied the water by failing to stick to their own conditions. It was they who had insisted that the school could be improved by the addition of a qualified assistant. Now they had dropped that condition and furthermore were allowing Stevenson himself to define the situation – a situation which was getting more and more out of their control.

Autumn of 1844 saw another Dick Bequest Trust inspection of Kemnay school. Again the findings were unsatisfactory, but since Stevenson had shown some willingness to improve the school, the Trustees agreed not to press the matter of a qualified assistant. Instead, they indicated their concern by reducing his allowance to 'a scale very inferior to what ought to have been obtained by the teacher of a school possessing the advantages of Kemnay'. (Dick Bequest Trust minute 1851 – SRO ref. GD1/4/4) One can only assume that such a measure would be unlikely to induce Stevenson to take on the extra expense of a new assistant teacher.

It seems incredible but, after all the controversy surrounding the teaching methods at Kemnay which had placed it under the microscope of inspection between 1842–4, there was now to be a gap of five years before the school was inspected again by the Dick Trustees. This prolonged omission was rather feebly explained as the result of 'the more than usually numerous changes of incumbencies in the parish schools' after 1843 and the need to inspect these as a priority. Why it did not occur to the Trustees to appoint another inspector to ease the load on Menzies, is a mystery. Furthermore, having pronounced Stevenson 'guilty' of running an unsatisfactory school and having 'fined' him by cutting his allowance, the Trustees afforded the accused no opportunity over a five year stretch to demonstrate his reformed character! Not that Stevenson was inclined to bend to the whims of the Trustees – the fact that his allowance remained at the reduced level over the five year period would only have served to heighten the sense of injustice he felt about his treatment at the hands of the Dick Bequest Trustees. The five year gap may also have inclined him to think that he had 'got off the hook' i.e. that the stipulation about hiring a qualified assistant had been dropped – not so!

Kemnay school was inspected again on 13 August 1849, this time with three gentlemen in attendance – Mr Young, Mr Menzies and Mr Morrison. Little seemed to have changed at the school, as far as the inspectors were concerned. Apart from the pleasant surroundings and fine school buildings, the report on the visit contains a catalogue of indictments on Stevenson's methods including:

> Stevenson's questioning technique was faulty. Some questions by their very nature suggested the answers – others were very superficial, feeble or trifling, not requiring deep thought or reflection by the pupils.

> He was not stretching the pupils, who seemed to be capable of more. His most advanced pupils were 'mere children' compared to younger pupils in other schools – 'this appears to us to be unpardonably bad'.

> His questioning of pupils was the worst that the inspectors had seen on that particular tour of schools.

> His English lesson on Etymology could have been good if he had put it to its proper use. However, 'there is no attempt of this sort here, and the use made of these Exercises would be ludicrous if it were not melancholy… This is certainly very miserable teaching'.

> There were too few written exercises in Arithmetic.
> Stevenson was anxious not to exhibit his Latin pupils.

The inspectors concluded with the following damning statement that:

'...there is no foundation of solid learning here, either in the dead languages or in English; and it appears now to be manifest that neither Mr Stevenson nor his present Assistant (Mr Emslie) is capable of teaching in a sound and instructive manner'.

Another part of the concluding remarks is worthy of mention here because it gives an insight into the thinking of the Dick Bequest Trustees. They praise the school building whose 'appearance is very remarkable', the 'charms of the situation of the school' and 'Mr Stevenson's art in gratifying the taste'. All these have 'contributed to confer upon it considerable celebrity derived from the impressions made upon tourists'. Undoubtedly, this last remark refers to an article on Stevenson and Kemnay school which appeared in Chamber's Edinburgh Journal in January 16, 1841 (reproduced on p32 – 37). However, they go on to say that they 'regard it , therefore, as a source of concern and matter of deep regret, that a seminary offering pretensions so great, and of which the attractions are in many respects very seductive, must be pronounced entirely defective in whatever constitutes a well taught school'.

Reading between the lines, the Trustees were really more concerned about the education given to the 17 boarders than to the 84 parish pupils. The boarders required the sort of academic education for University that Stevenson was just not capable of providing. Stevenson had no formal academic qualifications – he was a self-made man who had used his initiative, dedication and large amounts of his own money, to build a fine school. Its ornamentation and layout, the garden tended by the pupils, the school orchestra all gave the impression that this was a school of distinction. A tourist had been taken in by the outward trappings of the place and that person's article further portrayed Kemnay as a highly desirable establishment to send one's well-to-do offspring to obtain a quality education. It was now the duty of the Trustees to ensure that wealthy parents were not 'seduced' into sending their children to an inferior academy. After all, the well-to-do should expect solid educational instruction, the heart of which was a good grounding in Latin and Greek, English grammar and literature, mathematics and science. How was Stevenson going to prepare his boarders for University if he lacked such a background and was very weak on grammar and the classics?

On the 12th September 1849, Menzies wrote to Stevenson itemising some of the faults found at the inspection. Unless he was prepared to employ an assistant of good education, his fund would be cut off altogether. At this point, the 'hidden agenda' of the welfare of his middle class boarders also came out into the open when Menzies admitted that the Trustees were driven to this conclusion 'on account of the respectable rank of many of your pupils'. The Trustees seemed to be more concerned with Stevenson's own private boarding establishment rather than with the parish school. Whether the Trustees were in fact outwith their own jurisdiction by interfering in Stevenson's private domain is difficult to discern from Dick's will. Certainly, the Garioch Presbytery Committee seemed to think so. They objected to 'the incompetence of the Trustees to deal with Mr Stevenson as they seemed to wish to do upon any matter peculiar to his Boarding Establishment, Mr Dick's will confining their attention to Parish Schools'.

Menzies sent a copy of the letter to the Rev. George Peter asking him to approve and second the suggestion made to Stevenson about getting an assistant. Peter wrote back saying that he opposed and resented the actions of the Dick Bequest. As we will see, the local minister, backed up by the Garioch Presbytery, supported the work that Stevenson was doing at the school. To make matters worse, the Presbytery had themselves been inspecting the school (favourably) every year and sending their reports to the Dick Trustees. It is understandable therefore that the minister should feel strongly about the way the Trustees were handling this affair. As far as he was concerned, they had taken absolutely no cognizance of the previous five years of favourable reports faithfully sent in by the Garioch Presbytery.

Why was there such a gulf between the views of the Trustees and the local Presbytery over the merits of Stevenson's academy? Although it never formed part of the debate, it seems clear that each of these bodies was looking at the school from a different perspective. From the professorial heights of the Dick Bequest Trust in Edinburgh, they saw it as their mission to elevate the literary and academic character of schools and their teachers and Kemnay was a prime target because of the select boarding element who were expected to receive a traditional academic grounding. However, from the lowlier level of the parish minister and his committee, their sights were set on the more practical business of providing a basic education for the local populace for the four or five years that they would attend the school. This would involve the three R's and religious instruction. Anything more than that was a bonus. The fact that Stevenson did all this and more, as well as extending and improving the school buildings out of his own pocket, afforded him great respect and admiration amongst the local people. It was a mystery to them how such a dynamic and committed figure as Stevenson could now be having his Dick allowance withdrawn.

Another 18 months elapsed before any further steps were taken to resolve the dispute. The committee of Garioch Presbytery submitted a glowing report on Kemnay school in March 1851. Because it was at such variance with the Trustees' stated position, they decided to make a special inspection of the school two months later. Whether by design or accident, the letter intimating the Trustees' intention to visit Stevenson had not reached him by the time the inspection party arrived. As it was, Stevenson was caught unawares and his assistant, Mr Emslie was in Aberdeen for the morning. Menzies was accompanied by Dr. Pyper, Professor of Humanities at St. Andrews University and formerly a teacher at the High School of Edinburgh and Professor MacDougall of Edinburgh University and formerly a teacher at the Edinburgh Academy. Pyper and MacDougall were at pains to explain that they had been as impartial as they could be in examining the school, which took all of five hours. Their subsequent report was written up three days later (9th May). It contained both positive and negative points:

In its favour they noted,

'Few things can be more prepossessing or tasteful than the grounds, decorations, and entire appearance of Kemnay School' and 'the manner in which the whole has been laid out is in the highest degree creditable to the taste of Mr Stevenson'.

'The conduct of the scholars throughout the day was certainly most orderly'.

'The spelling in the upper half of the (English) class seemed respectable'.

'On the ...most prominent facts in the history of the Patriarchs, of the Israelites, and in part also of our Saviour's life, the class answered both readily and respectably'.

'For the purpose of getting at the meaning and relations of the several clauses (in the highest English class), a simple and good expedient was resorted to by the teacher...'

'The examination in Geography was conducted by Mr Emslie the Assistant. It was necessarily brief …but it was carried on with much spirit, and with results highly satisfactory and creditable'.

'The Penmanship was very superior, and entitled to the highest praise'.

As criticism, they point out,

'The reading was very slovenly, being defective in distinctness and accuracy, to say nothing of expression or intelligence'.

'…in everything that concerned grammar, etymology, construction, analysis, or explanation, their grounding, if any, appeared to be of the most imperfect description'.

Mr Stevenson's own mode of examination seemed to us sadly inefficient, being scarcely fitted in any measure to exercise the mental facilities or to stimulate the interest of the pupils'.

'Mr Stevenson's examination of the contents of the passage (in the second English class) was singularly superficial, desultory, and unsatisfactory. His questions were in general either leading ones, or quite trivial and puerile'.

'In all (the) English classes we could not help remarking the lack of interest, alacrity, and animation'.

'Mr Stevenson took no part in the examination of either Latin class. He showed much solicitude to avoid this duty, and pressed it anxiously on the visitors. The same is true as regards the examination of the highest class in English'.

Armed with this independent assessment of Kemnay school which seemed to confirm the main points made by Menzies on his visit in September 1849, the Trustees now considered that their decision to cut off Stevenson's allowance had been vindicated. As far as the Garioch Presbytery was concerned though, the matter was by no means closed. They wrote back to the Trustees on the 28th November 'using the language of menace' and asking for a conference to resolve the dispute. If the Trustees refused, the

Presbytery threatened to publish their complaints about the alleged injustice done to Stevenson. The Trustees replied that although they agreed to the conference, they were not prepared to change the decision they had come to. On hearing this, the Presbytery saw no point in going on with any further discussions and set about compiling their own counter-blast against the Trustees. In it, the Presbytery set out their objections in some detail, of which the following are the main points:

Complaints about the Trustees' document

The principal objection here was that the Trustees had suppressed information which was unfavourable to their own case as well as withholding any evidence which cast Stevenson in a good light. For example, no direct reference is made to the Chamber's Journal article which had praised Stevenson's school to the hilt. Neither did they mention the awkward fact that the Milne Bequest, which had similar aims to the Dick Bequest, rated Stevenson very highly. They had ranked Kemnay in the top out of 10 classes of merit into which Aberdeenshire schools were placed.

Complaints about Menzies

The Garioch Presbytery were particularly scathing about Mr Menzies' qualifications for the job of school inspector. For most of the year, Menzies was a 'Scotch attorney' – 'a profession which gave him no preparation for being a judge of school teaching; and that, though he had some acquaintance with the writings of theorists upon education, he never had any experience in school teaching, but that he inspected the schools of the three counties merely as an employment for the summer leisure allowed him by his profession'. (Another Communication to the Presbyteries within the Counties of Aberdeen, Banff, and Moray, being observations on that made by the Trustees of the Dick Bequest regarding the Case of Kemnay, etc. etc. p11) During these months, he was only able to visit about one third of the 141 schools in the Dick Bequest area and because of the great pressure on his time, each visit was of necessity curtailed to little more than an hour on average. For this meagre service, Menzies was paid a princely £210 per annum. This was just a part-time job which gave Menzies almost three times the annual salary of a north-east parish schoolmaster. The Presbytery Committee pointed out that Menzies was not very good value for his money compared to the Milne Bequest inspector, Dr. Cruickshank who received only £150 in salary and expenses and he visited 100 schools every year.

Another complaint was that Menzies' ability to perform his duties as an inspector was also hindered, they claimed, by his 'defective hearing'. Apparently, he was in the habit of using an ear-trumpet at his place of worship in Edinburgh. However, whilst at Kemnay on inspection business, he did not use a hearing aid and as a result, pupils had to repeat answers given for his benefit and his 'angry-like voice' tended to frighten 'timid children into silence'. (Correspondence between a Committee of the Presbytery of Garioch and the Trustees of the Dick Bequest respecting the Parish School of Kemnay p26)

Complaints about the 1849 Inspection

Menzies visited Kemnay at the beginning of harvest-time – entirely the wrong time of year to see the school working to its full capacity. It was quite normal and acceptable, in the days before compulsory education, for the older pupils to help gather in the crops, but this also meant that most of the schoolwork in evidence at this time would be fairly elementary. If inspected, the schoolmaster would not be able to demonstrate the work of higher learning available to the upper school. When Dr. Woodford, Her Majesty's Inspector of Schools came upon Kemnay at harvest-time, he hesitated to form 'any decided opinion of the efficiency with which the several branches were taught'. (Another Communication to the Presbyteries within the Counties of Aberdeen, Banff, and Moray, being observations on that made by the Trustees of the Dick Bequest regarding the Case of Kemnay, etc. etc. p9)

Another complaint levelled at Menzies concerned his method of inspection. Unlike the Milne Bequest inspectors, who actually observed and made a judgment on the teaching abilities of the schoolmaster in the classroom, Menzies preferred to look at the teacher's skills of examining pupils i.e. asking them questions to discover how much they knew about lessons done a few days before. He had been influenced, they contended, by the 'got-up exhibitions of question and answer' which went on at the Circus Place School in Edinburgh during its public open days. The Presbytery Committee argued that this kind of showmanship was unrepresentative of the kind of activities that normally went on during a typical day in the parish school. Furthermore, not all teachers were suited by temperament to putting on a display in front of visiting strangers – 'a trial under which many teachers habitually, and Mr Stevenson among others, make an inferior appearance, from constitutional causes'. In other words, Stevenson was put at a disadvantage because he became nervous and performed badly in front of the inspectors.

Reports on schools visited by the Dick Bequest inspector were normally confidential and for the eyes of the Trustees only. However, because of the complaints over the case of Kemnay, the Trustees had been forced to justify their decisions and that meant publication of the 1849 and 1851 reports. The Garioch Presbytery were now able to find out exactly what Menzies had thought of Stevenson. Of course, we have already seen that Menzies feared that the 'seductive charms' of the grounds and buildings of Kemnay school might lead potential clients to believe that it was a better institution than it actually was. Not unnaturally, the Presbytery took exception to the implication that Stevenson was some kind of educational charlatan. They were particularly concerned that Menzies opinion could have found its way into a confidential report which Stevenson had no way of being able to refute.

Complaints about the 1851 Inspection

First of all, the Presbytery Committee alleged that the special visit conducted by MacDougall and Pyper in 1851 was biased; their report on Kemnay school 'bears upon the face of it grounds which prevent its being regarded as of the value of a separate testimony, and which give it much of the character of an instructed corroboration of the evidence of (Menzies)'. This seems a rather flimsy criticism as the only evidence the Presbytery were able to muster against the two Professors was that they had read Menzies 1849 report on Stevenson and therefore had their 'minds possessed beforehand'. The fact that the Professors said they would dismiss from their minds what had been communicated to them and that they would only base their report on observation at the school, was discounted because 'the matter and the expression of their Report irresistibly show that they have not succeeded'. (Another Communication to the Presbyteries within the Counties of Aberdeen, Banff, and Moray, being observations on that made by the Trustees of the Dick Bequest regarding the Case of Kemnay, etc. etc. p20) The Report was supposed to be 'written under a bias' because of 'a marked unwillingness to give praise'!

But surely if the Professors observed little of merit in Kemnay school, lack of praise should have been expected to come through in the final report. In fact, we have already seen that there were at least seven positive points made about the school by MacDougall and Pyper even although they did seem to corroborate most of Menzies criticisms, if in less harsh tones.

Complaints about the administration of the Dick Bequest Trust

The Presbytery Committee took great pleasure in discovering that the Trustees had been awarding Stevenson almost the maximum allowance annually from the inception of the Bequest back in 1832, right up to 1841. Then within a year, and after Menzies had inspected the school, Stevenson had become so inefficient that he needed to take on a qualified assistant! How could two such diametrically opposed assessments emanate from the same body over such a short space of time?

Between 1844 and 1849, no inspection was made of Kemnay school despite the fact that it had been condemned as an inefficient school. The Trustees gave as their reason for the 5 year gap the need to visit new schoolmasters appointed since 1843. Why was it then that Menzies still managed to visit established teachers in the vicinity of Kemnay during this time? And when he did visit in 1849, it was at the wrong time of year (harvest time) and only for about an hour and a half – hardly enough time for a thorough inspection. Furthermore, no account was taken of the five annual reports sent in to the Trustees by the Garioch Presbytery. On the request of the Dick Bequest, local Presbytery Committees had been asked to inspect and report on their local schools and to provide these annual reports to the Trustees as 'a principal source of their information as to the condition of schools and as giving them a degree of confidence and satisfaction' in distributing the Funds. (Another Communication to the Presbyteries within the Counties of Aberdeen, Banff, and Moray, being observations on that made by the Trustees of the Dick Bequest regarding the Case of Kemnay, etc. etc. p10)

The Garioch Presbytery were understandably upset that their consistently glowing reports on Stevenson were being ignored, especially as for a five year period, the only information the Trustees had on the work going on at school came from the Presbytery. Unlike Menzies visits, the Presbytery Committee inspected the school at a time when the school had a full complement of pupils so that all branches of the school's work could be looked at.

Evidence in support of Stevenson

Whatever the Dick Trustees might say, the public in and around Kemnay certainly supported Stevenson. After all, he had used up to £1,200 of his own money to extend and improve the parish school which had been 'but a thatched and smoky hut' when he first took up the post. His predecessor, Dawson, never had more than 50 pupils attending the school and latterly that number had dropped to around 20. Now, in the early 1850's, Stevenson had taken that figure up to around 100 pupils and boarders. (These figures are at odds with those given in the New Statistical Account which claimed there were around 130 parish children and 30 boarders in 1842.) The Trustees own figures showed how popular Kemnay was in the locality. The average attendance at schools throughout the Dick Bequest area was 12.8% of the population whereas for Kemnay parish school alone i.e. not including the boarders, the figure was 16.7%. Surely this was a clear indication that the local people had confidence in Stevenson as a schoolmaster? The boarding school also provided ample evidence of public support due to 'the unusually long duration of his Boarding Academy – its having been attended of late years chiefly by the sons of relatives or acquaintances of former pupils from all parts of the country, both in the immediate neighbourhood and at a distance. (Another Communication to the Presbyteries within the Counties of Aberdeen, Banff, and Moray, being observations on that made by the Trustees of the Dick Bequest regarding the Case of Kemnay, etc. etc. p8)

It seems incredible nowadays that a dispute over the merits of one schoolmaster in a small parish school could have raged on for over 10 years. However, having laid out the detailed arguments, we can probably begin to see how and why the case of Kemnay school became so embittered and immune to negotiated settlement. First of all, there was probably a personality clash between Stevenson and Menzies which would have been simmering on for many years. The *Aberdeen Journal* even went as far as to suggest that there existed an 'ancient grudge' between the two. Reading Menzies' confidential reports on Stevenson, one does detect an underlying disdain – after all, Menzies was a highly educated and qualified professor of law, whereas Stevenson had no formal education other than of the parish variety. Despite this 'handicap' though, and by dedication and hard work, he had managed to elevate the school from an educational backwater to a notable Scottish seminary. Whether Menzies resented the self-made man's success is difficult to say, but he clearly was concerned that Stevenson should not inadvertently be giving the impression that his school had good academic credentials when the inspections showed Stevenson to be very weak on the classics and English grammar.

Throughout the years when the dispute was battling on, there was also a sense in which the two sides were talking at cross-purposes. The Trustees were bound by the terms of the Bequest to safeguard and raise the literary character of schools. For most schoolmasters i.e. those who were not original participators in the Bequest, this meant undergoing trial by examination – eleven hours of written exam papers to complete over a two day period if they were to gain an allowance.

Stevenson, of course, escaped this gruelling test and perhaps the Trustees felt they had thereby missed an opportunity to 'find him out' – hence the 'harsh' treatment meted out during Menzies' visits. Whatever the case may be, Stevenson failed to come up to the academic standards set by the Trustees. At the local level though, the Garioch Presbytery had a different way of judging success. It is interesting to note that in all the 47 pages of detailed rebuttals of the Trustees case, nowhere did they try to defend Stevenson on his ability to teach Latin and English grammar at the highest level in the school. Instead, they took a more comparative approach i.e. Kemnay was a good school because it had a higher than average ratio of pupils per head of population and also had a high ranking compared to other schools according to the Milne Bequest method of assessment.

The Trustees, on the other hand, were bound by the terms of the Bequest to elevate the 'literary character of schools'. Unfortunately Dick died before he was able to spell out in detail what he meant by this phrase. Consequently, that is all the Trustees had to go on as a guide for Menzies during his visits to schools. If both the Trustees and the Presbytery Committee had been clearer as to what it was that Dick sought in north-east schoolmasters, then some sort of compromise might have been reached. As it was, both sides were able to marshal a great deal of evidence to support their own point of view on Stevenson's merits or demerits and a prolonged dialogue of the deaf ensued. We should not be surprised either at the lengths to which the local Presbytery Committee were prepared to go to support Stevenson. After all, he had done more than any other schoolmaster to raise the quality of education at Kemnay. Furthermore, they were not about to abandon a man who had put most, if not all, of his earnings into improving and extending the school buildings.

One must also have sympathy for Stevenson. He had to fight a long war of attrition against the Dick Trustees, with his own reputation at stake and latterly, his name and Kemnay school featuring prominently in the local press. The *Aberdeen Journal* itself recognised what could happen: "It speedily becomes known in the parish and throughout the district that the schoolmaster has been condemned. The parent of every dull child ...has the opinion, which he, of course always entertained, confirmed. The schoolmaster feels that he cannot ...enter into a correspondence in his own defence; and it is well understood, that the expression of the Trustees...is an original sin for which there is no atonement'. (*Aberdeen Journal* 21.7.1852 p8)

On top of this, Stevenson's must have been the most thoroughly inspected school in Scotland at this time, what with the Dick Bequest, the Milne Bequest, the Committee of Garioch Presbytery and Her Majesty's Inspectors all trooping through the school door. No wonder Stevenson had a delicate constitution when his methods were being put under the microscope so frequently. Certainly, he did not perform at his best under public scrutiny as these were 'circumstances likely to agitate him'.
(Another Communication to the Presbyteries within the Counties of Aberdeen, Banff, and Moray, being observations on that made by the Trustees of the Dick Bequest regarding the Case of Kemnay, etc. etc. p30)

Stevenson and the committee of the Presbytery found a ready ally in the editor of the *Aberdeen Journal*. Soon after the publication of the Presbytery's 'Another Communication' document, the local paper devoted considerable column space to publicising the case. While professing a 'desire to take an impartial view of the unfortunate difference', (*Aberdeen Journal* 12.5.1852) the paper proceeded to repeat the Presbytery's allegations without in any way balancing these with the Dick Bequest viewpoint. Stevenson also came in for some welcome praise: 'Mr Stevenson has for years stood high in the estimation of parents and guardians of youth as a most painstaking and industrious teacher, and he may congratulate himself upon one consequence of his having come under the censure of the Dick Trustees, as the knowledge of his having done so must have suggested to the Presbytery the necessity, for their own vindication, of a more than usually rigorous and thorough examination of his school, his method of teaching, and the success attending it, which has resulted in most favourable reports'. (*Aberdeen Journal* ibid)
By the end of the article, the editor had set aside his impartiality and pronounced the Trustees guilty: 'Now that the system of inspection adopted

by the Dick Trustees has been found insufficient, and may, if the wish exists, become, in the hands of their inspector, an instrument of oppression, we have every confidence that the Trustees will, without delay, apply the remedy necessary to cure the evil'. (*Aberdeen Journal* ibid) Of course, the paper was suggesting that Menzies should be sacked and Stevenson reinstated to the Bequest.

Taking advantage of the local press sympathy, an anonymous source put a notice in the *Aberdeen Journal* on 14th July, 1852 berating the management of the Dick Bequest. There is little doubt that Stevenson and/or some of the other injured schoolmasters placed the notice. In it, they make two complaints against the Trustees:

Firstly, that they had departed from Dick's primary intention of supplementing the 'very trifling' salaries of teachers and that they were now giving 'extravagantly' to some, inadequately to others and nothing to a considerable amount of north-east teachers.

Secondly, that they had wasted Dick Bequest funds (against Dick's will) e.g. by paying for an Inspector of Schools and his expenses and by inspecting schoolmasters in Edinburgh.

By going against Dick's will, the Trustees 'whole proceedings, by such unwarranted transactions, are invalidated, void, and null'. The notice called on other dissatisfied schoolmasters to meet together a fortnight hence when a petition to Parliament would be drawn up. In advance to the meeting, the complainants suggested that Parliament should be asked:

    to inquire into the operations of the Dick Bequest Trust.

    to recompense schoolmasters who had suffered at the hands of the Trustees (especially those who had been withdrawn from the Fund).

    to sack the current Trustees and appoint others.

What the exact sequence of events was after July 1852, is not known, but according to the Trustees, Stevenson printed and circulated a petition on his own. However, the final version of the petition was by Stevenson and three other schoolmasters – Mr Norrie of Insch, Mr Mann of Premnay, and Mr Cooper of Meldrum school. It was presented to Parliament on the 6th

December, 1852. Another source says that the petition was read out by the Duke of Richmond in the House of Lords.

All of this apparently was to no avail. The Trustees and the system for supervising schools remained in place. At the height of the controversy, the Dick Bequest minutes reveal that Menzies did offer to give up his post, but his resignation was not accepted. In the following year, 1853, Menzies even took on the additional post of Treasurer on the death of the incumbent. He continued to carry out his duties as Visitor of schools until his death in 1856. The Trustees had lost, according to one historian 'a man of great firmness and prudence'. (Rev. Dr. William Paul in 'Past and Present of Aberdeenshire' p87)

Information about Stevenson on the education front begins to fade away after the Dick Bequest affair, but he still retained an active interest in community life. There is no record of when he was appointed Session clerk, possibly when he took up the post of Schoolmaster, but he was ordained to the Eldership on December 12th 1841, and the following day he was appointed representative elder to both Synod and Presbytery. This position he held for some two years. At the first meeting of the Parochial Board on October 28th 1845, Andrew Stevenson is recorded as being Elder and Session Clerk.

A fund had been in existence for many years, the interest of which was annually paid to the Schoolmaster. This fund amounted to 850 Merks Scots (valued in 1850 at £47 4s 5d sterling). On December 20th 1850:

> '...£2 15s 7d was added at this date by Andrew Stevenson Esqre. Kemnay Parish School and Academy, to the Mortification of 850 Merks Scots in order to make up that sum to £50 sterling in all time coming for behoof of himself and Successors in office.'

For many years the care of the poor had been the responsibility of the Church. The necessary funding for this was derived from church collections, income from the letting of church pews, donations received annually from the heritors of the parish kirk, Lord Kintore and Burnett of Kemnay. The kirk also derived interest from invested funds. These had been accumulated over the years by judicious management of their own funds and by bequests. By the mid nineteenth century the capital amounted to £400.

All this was due to change. In 1845 was passed an Act for the Amendment and better Administration of Laws relating to the Relief of the Poor in Scotland. This transferred the relief of the poor from the kirk to a Parochial Board consisting of up to thirty members and including four representatives of the Kirk Session. The duties of the Board included making up a roll of the Poor, appointing a Poor Inspector, raising funds by assessment and making a Roll of Ratepayers, making exemption of those unable to pay and setting up and regulating Poorhouses and Hospitals. All parish property was vested in the Parochial Board though Church collections were still disposed of by the church. The Kirk Session continued to disburse funds to the poor until February 1850, when a meeting was called to consider raising an assessment in the parish as their own funds had decreased to £100 which they wished to keep for emergencies such as crop failure or other such calamity in the parish. The heritors would not agree to an assessment until the funds were exhausted, which happened later that year.

The Poor Inspector elected in 1850 was Alexander Hadden Emslie, assistant to Andrew Stevenson, Schoolmaster, and it was he who was responsible for collecting all the necessary information required to raise funding through an assessment on tenants and heritors.

At the meeting of the Parochial Board held on 27th June 1854, Emslie resigned his office as he was leaving the district. Andrew Stevenson, who had been chairman since 1851 immediately resigned that post, in order to take up the position of interim Inspector. On the 5th August 1854, this appointment was ratified and Stevenson said that he would take no more than had been paid previously viz. £10 as Inspector and £8 as Collector. He intimated to the Board that since his appointment in June he had visited all the paupers in the parish and within five miles. He also pointed out that the Poor law manual possessed by the Board was somewhat outdated, and suggested that they purchase a copy of 'Dunlop's new Manual of the Poor Law.'

At a meeting of the Parochial Board held on 17th May 1856, Andrew Stevenson laid his books before the Board where they were examined and found correct. We read that the 'debt was reduced to £18 11s 3¼d which sum Mr Stevenson advanced out of his own pocket until the assessment could be collected'.

On 21st February 1857: "...laid before the Board all books in connection with the Inspector's Office – requested the newly elected members to come and examine and that he would explain everything. They, however, declined to do so but requested the Inspector to publish what they called a "Statement or paperie" which he said he would do after the 14th May although he was not sure he was obliged to do so by the act. The Board then distributed to the Poor which after some obstinate debating by one of the newly elected members was accomplished."

Andrew Stevenson died in June of that year before, we believe, he had time to produce that 'paperie'. George Ogg, the assistant Inspector, was appointed interim Inspector, and on applying to the Town and County Bank, Inverury, for funds to make the August distribution, the withdrawal was disallowed as there was money due to the Bank. The matter was handed over to legal advisors who found several discrepancies, but the Board as a body was exonerated. There was a certain amount of aggression between the ratepayers and members of the School Parochial Board, but in time this died down. The Board eventually wrote off the debt, which amounted to just over £54. Whether they were able to reclaim it from Stevenson's estate is not recorded.

1855 saw the introduction of compulsory registration of births, marriages and deaths, and on 10th October 1854, Andrew Stevenson had been appointed Registrar.

A gravestone was erected in his memory in Kemnay Churchyard, paid for by some of his friends. The picturesque school buildings lasted just a few more years than their creator. The whole lot was demolished and a new school and schoolhouse erected in 1860.

Andrew Stevenson's character and influence were later summed up by Dr John Davidson of Inverurie Parish Church, reminiscing in the 1880's after a ministry of some forty years in Inverurie:

"...a nook which forty years ago, contained nothing but a slovenly set of farm buildings and a picturesque parish school; presided over by a corresponding school-master, who wore a glossy black wig ringleted, a suit of black with ample shirt front, and dress shoes. Mr Stevenson, with nothing beyond a parish school training and ability to make much of it, had developed his school by teaching subjects beyond the elementary branches (other than the classics) into what had come to be called "The Kemnay Academy". About 1844 it was in esteem among rising farmers and parents who wanted to settle their sons in a commercial kind of school; and for the accommodation of his clients, Mr Stevenson had bit by bit extended his miserably small low-roofed thatched parish schoolroom, by wooden erections tastefully outlined, till the whole made a sight deemed worthy of the sketcher's art. Poor man, his expenditure upon extending and ornamenting his pretty erections, and also entertaining in the way of business, ruined him; these being paid for not out of revenue altogether, and leaving him seriously in debt, when his 'academy' came to the end of the short life that such institutions enjoy."

Perhaps a fitting memorial to Andrew Stevenson can be found in W. Cadenhead's poem 'Kemnay Revisited' from which the following is taken:

> But alas! and dule! and dule!
> The dear, sweet, bonnie skule.
> > That was a'thing to me ance at Kemnay,
> It was levell'd wi' the ground,
> And nae trace was to be found
> > O' the cosiest and kindest hame in Kemnay.

> Within the kirkyard lone
> There was graved upon a stone
> > A name that had a coothie power in Kemnay;
> And beneath a grassy heap
> There was mouldering in its sleep
> > The kindest heart that ever beat in Kemnay.

("Ingatherings" – W. Cadenhead p125)

The advertisement below appeared in the *Aberdeen Journal*.

Sale of Household Furniture, &c.,
AT
SCHOOL - HOUSE OF KEMNAY.

There will be exposed for sale, by public roup, on TUESDAY the 18th day of August,

THE whole EFFECTS which belonged to the late Mr Andrew Stevenson, Schoolmaster, Kemnay—consisting of an Eight-day Clock and Time Piece—Mahogany, Fir, and Hardwood Tables and Dressers—Mahogany and Hardwood Hair-bottomed Chairs—Feather Beds and Pillows—a large quantity of Blankets and Bed and Table Linen—a number of Musical Instruments, comprising a Pianoforte, almost new, a Seraphim, an Organ, and a most valuable selection of Tenor and Bass Violins—Four-post and Tent beds, with curtains—Glass fronted and other Presses—Grates, Fenders, and Fire-irons—German Silver Dessert and Tea Spoons—German Silver Dividers and Toddy Ladles—Knives and Forks—Paintings and Prints—a well-selected and extensive Library, to be arranged in Lots—China, Glass, and Stoneware, along with a general Assortment of Culinary Articles.

As the Lots will be numerous, the Sale will commence at Ten, A.M. precisely.

JOHN ELRICK, Auctioneer.

The following article is re-printed from *Chambers Edinburgh Journal* 16th January 1841. It also gives considerable insight into Andrew Stevenson and the school he had developed by that time:

"The Parish school of Kemnay has been made known to us by the merest accident: we have not seen it, nor ever had the slightest intercourse or correspondence with anyone connected with it. In now introducing it to notice, we must be considered as animated solely by a wish to make the public acquainted with something which we believe will interest them, and to present to the humbler class of rural teachers an example which seems worthy of being followed. There are, of course, throughout the country, many seminaries of more important character, and which equally merit being celebrated. The reader will, nevertheless, understand what it is which makes one sometimes admire the simple wild flower more than the cultivated denizens of the parterre: and he will soon see that, in the remoteness and obscurity of Kemnay, and the union of enterprise and intelligence with perseverance which has overcome these disadvantages, there is a claim upon his notice which he might be apt to dispute with regard to a much more imposing establishment.

A lady with whom we have the honour to be acquainted chanced in August last to pay a visit to a friend residing in Inverury, in Aberdeenshire. After every object within walking distance had been walked to, and when *ennui* was beginning to steal over the mind of the stranger, her entertainer proposed that they should have a drive to a country school, five miles off, where she had a son placed for his education as a boarder with a teacher. "Kemnay School, you must know," said the Inverury lady, "is no common parish school. It is under the care of an amiable enthusiast in education, who has done wonders in the place, and is beginning to attract attention in distant quarters. He is, I assure you, respected where he is known." "By all means, then, let us visit Kemnay School." said our friend.

The particulars of the visit were communicated in a letter, from which the following is an extract:

"Our way was for some time alongside the Don. We then left the river, and passed for some miles through a country generally barren, till at length we descended upon Kemnay, which appeared to me quite as a green spot in the wilderness. I could imagine no simple rural scene possessed of greater beauty than what was presented by the little group of cottages constituting the parish school establishment, planted as they are upon somewhat irregular ground, which for some distance around has been laid out with good taste, and exhibits a variety of fine green shrubs.

A few years ago the school and schoolhouse were, as usual in Scotland, merely a couple of cottages in juxtaposition. Mr Stevenson, the present teacher, has added one building after another, till it is now a considerable place. His last addition was a pretty large schoolroom, which is constructed of timber, pitched on the top. One must not wonder at the buildings not being of a very lasting kind, for not only has the teacher had to do all at his own expense, but he has done it with the certainty that all will become public property when he dies or leaves his situation. The place, nevertheless, seems sufficiently comfortable. The new erections have been made as the views of the teacher, respecting the duties of his charge, expanded, and as his boarding pupils became more numerous. After all, these are as yet only nineteen.

Generally, if there is a little garden for common vegetables near a Scottish parish school, it is all that is to be expected. Here there is a remarkably neat garden, situated on a piece of undulating ground, comprising a pretty piece of water in a serpentine form; while the ground immediately round the new schoolroom is laid out in shrubbery and flower borders, with seats and arbours, the whole being in a style which might not shame a gentleman's mansion. I have never seen finer vegetables, or eaten more delicious fruit, than I did here. Judge my surprise when I was told that the whole is the result of the labours of the children, who are thus taught a useful and tasteful art, and at the same time engaged in a physical recreation highly conducive to their health. My curiosity was excited to know how their labours were conducted. The garden and the ground, I understand, are divided into compartments, and so many boys are attached to each. These companies, as they are called, have each a separate set of tools, all of which are kept in the nicest order and arrangement in a small wooden house erected for the purpose.

It was singular, you will allow, at a time when industrial education is only beginning to be thought of in England, to find it practised on a large scale, and under the best regulations, in a remote and barren part of the northern county of Aberdeen. I was taken from the garden to a carpentry workshop, where the boys everyday exercise themselves in the ingenious trade of the joiner. They make part of the school furniture, seats for the garden and shrubbery, and many other useful articles.

We were now conducted into the schoolroom, which I found to be a spacious apartment, fitted with all conveniences of blackboards etc. as in the most improved schools in Edinburgh, with the addition of something which I had never seen in any similar place, namely, a variety of musical instruments hung upon the walls. I found only the boarders present, for the day was the last of the week, and all the native pupils had been dismissed, at the usual early hour, to their homes. Mr Stevenson, nevertheless, gave us a small specimen of a concert. Some boys took flutes, others violins, and one or two violas or violoncellos; Mr Stevenson also took his instrument and assumed the office of leader. I then heard several pieces of music, amongst which were some sacred pieces performed in a manner really astonishing, when the ages of the musicians were considered. I may mention that Mr Stevenson is himself a good musician and even a composer. The boys are of all parts from six to nineteen, and several of them are from distant parts of the world. Many have made considerable progress in drawing, and in the copying of maps.

The author, as I may call him, of the extraordinary scene with which I was now so delighted, is an unmarried middle-aged man of gentle and benevolent character. Reared in humble circumstances, in the parish where he now teaches, he had not even the universal privilege of the Scottish peasantry, that of receiving the elements of knowledge at school. He had, however, a natural thirst for learning, and, after experiencing considerable difficulties, he was fortunate enough to attract the regard of the amiable pastor of the parish, the late Dr. Mitchell, who was so much interested in his character as to take it upon himself the trouble of teaching him, which he persisted in doing until the young man was fitted to proceed to college. When about to take the latter step, the parish school, which had been inefficiently taught for no less than seventy years, became vacant, and he felt it as a proud moment when the place became his, with a salary of twenty six pounds. He took home with him his aged parents, and commenced his duties as a teacher, with a mind eager to do its best, but hampered by the defects of his own education, to overcome which was not the least difficulty he had to contend with. From one thing he went on to another, every improvement in education found in him one willing to try it. He proceeded upon the monitorial plan for some time, but for various reasons now only uses it occasionally. He was, however, and still is, a faithful adherent of the intellectual mode of teaching. In time, he began to add to his course; drawing being amongst the first of the new branches. After twenty years, his little seminary has expanded to what I have described it to be. That the prompting cause of all these exertions is neither ambition nor the love of gain, the whole circumstances go to prove; he is apparently animated by the enthusiasm of his profession. With no family round him to claim his regard, he lives entirely amongst and for his pupils. They are his daily friends and companions. He seeks no other society. Many of the poorer class of the parish children, whose parents are unable to pay even the usual school fees, small as these are, attend gratuitously, and receive all the benefits of the excellent system which good fortune has placed in their out-of-the-way locality. The teacher remembers how precious learning was to himself, when circumstances seemed to forbid that he should ever drink of the fount of knowledge.

We were now conducted to the eating room, where a meal was laid out for the master, his assistant, and the pupils, all at one table. This was a long room, composed, I think, of the original school and part of the schoolhouse thrown into one. At the head of the room was a piano-forte; at the bottom a stove. We had tea, an abundance of bread, and in considerable variety, in addition to butter, were honey and jellies, the two last being in compliment to the strangers. Observing a very little lad being placed at the foot of the table, and who said grace, I inquired if that was his ordinary situation and duty. I was informed that each boy takes to-day the place next below that which he had yesterday, so that they circulate round the table and experience each in his turn the advantages and duties of each situation. Even in this little arrangement I could see originality and superior understanding.

The assistant, who joined us at tea, is a young man in delicate health. I learned, in the course of a ramble through the house, that the master, in consideration of that circumstance, had lately given him his own room, for his better accommodation. The two gentlemen began to open their varied stores of information, and I could have willingly sat to listen to them for hours; but the evening was approaching, and we were obliged to take our leave.

Our readers will probably join us in thinking that there is something delightfully interesting, and even affecting, in this account of the doings of a good man. Good thus done in obscurity, with modesty, and for no object beyond itself – what can have greater claims upon general sympathy or praise? We almost fear to make it publicly known, lest being so, it become a hackneyed object of curiosity, and so lose the freshness and beauty connected with its present seclusion – lest, also, this worthy man should dislike to be brought so prominently before the world. If what we do is objectionable on these grounds, we would hope that the example will produce such good effects as to counterbalance all such drawbacks". (*Chambers Edinburgh Journal* 16.1.1841)

Andrew Stevenson
From a Painting by Stirling

George Proctor

George Proctor was born at Ardgrain, Ellon on June 19th 1830, where his father is variously described as cartwright and farmer. Little, in fact nothing, is known of George Proctor's early life, only that he graduated Master of Arts at Kings College, Aberdeen in March 1852.

He took over the Parochial School of Kemnay following the death of Andrew Stevenson in June 1857. The first mention we have of him is at a meeting of the Parochial Board of Kemnay held at the Schoolhouse on 9th November 1857 to elect a successor to the late Andrew Stevenson. George Proctor was unanimously elected as Registrar and Inspector of Poor and Collector of Poor's Assessment. Satisfactory security to the amount of £100 was a requirement for the Collector's appointment. The post of Registrar commanded a salary of £6 per annum, the others £5 each per annum. George Proctor accepted the post of Registrar as offered, but requested time to consider the other appointments. At the following meeting of the Board on 22nd November 1857, he 'informed the Board that he was prepared with security for his fidelity on intromission to the amount required but stated that he considered his providing such security entitled him to a more liberal salary as Collector and Inspector.' George Proctor accepted the increased offer of £6 per annum for each post.

He took on the posts of Poor Inspector and collector at a difficult time. As we have read in the previous chapter, there was found to be a discrepancy in the funds on the death of Andrew Stevenson. There is no doubt that this rankled some of the locals as we find several refusals 'to pay the present assessment until they receive an account for the year l4th May 1856 to l4th May 1857.' Although a document entitled 'Remarks on the Cash Accounts and Relative books kept by the late Mr Andrew Stevenson as Inspector of Poor and Collector, Parish of Kemnay' was read out to them, they were not to be placated.

The Board Minute of 9th January 1858 finishes with: 'It was seemingly resolved to give the objectors an abstract of the proceedings from May 1856 to May 1857.' Whether this was written at the time of the original minute or added later cannot now be deduced, but George Proctor called a meeting of the Board on 30th January 'for seeing about rectifying the matter concerning the objectors.' The meeting started with one member resigning from the Board. The Inspector is then accused of not carrying out all the wishes of the Board regarding notification of the objectors of the happenings to date and of not sending out the annual statement requested by them. 'The Inspector mentioned that he had at that time no abstract to give to the Objectors, and that the books belonging to the Parochial Board and Accounts were never rightly delivered over to the Inspector, as for instance Mr Ogg's account was never handed in to him until a few days ago. The Inspector also mentioned his intention to give up his offices of Inspector and Collector to the Board at the end of the quarter.' The minute is signed by Francis Carney. There follows:

> Schoolhouse Kemnay 2nd Feby 1858. There was no meeting of the Board today, none of the members having appeared. Mr Carney appeared and the late elected members Mr Malcolm and Mr Reid to settle the dispute mentioned in above minute. Mr Malcolm said Mr Carney was right, and Mr Reid did not know rightly about it. They differed from each other, but the Inspector agreed to put it now to the end of the minute in order to get it signed. The Inspector understands that Mr Carney called upon one at least of these two men before coming to the Schoolhouse. Note by the Inspector Geo. Proctor.

By the following meeting Mr Francis Carney had resigned as Chairman, but it appears that the resignation of the Inspector and Collector did not come about. It is difficult at this long distance in time to try and draw the full meaning of George Proctor's handling of the situation. Was he trying to exact his superior education and knowledge over these local farmers and tradesmen, or was he simply trying to keep his own nose clean in the matter?

The Parochial Board Minute of 13th November 1868 contains the following:

> The Chairman laid before the Board the report of Mr Alexr Campbell, General Superintendent of Poor on the Administration of the Poor Law in the Parish of Kemnay, which, through some oversight, had been neglected to be submitted to it at the previous meeting. After being read, it was ordered to be engrossed in the Minute. It ran as follows:
>
> "Parish of Kemnay
> Inspector Mr Geo Proctor visited 27th April 1868.

The Revised Roll should be engrossed in the Minutes. In the pay roll, the columns for allowances to paupers should be filled in and a reference given from Pay Roll to Day Cash Book for payments made for non-resident paupers.

The Day Cash Book should be closed on 14th May annually to agree with the return to the Board of Supervision: it should also be annually audited and docqueted as correct. The accounts do not appear to have been audited since 1860.
      Reported by
 (Signed) Alexr Campbell
      Genrl Superintendent May 13th 1868."

The Inspector stated then that these recommendations had been complied with. Whether the oversight was intentional or not we cannot tell.

All apparently went well until May 1875 when we read, 'The payment of the Collector of Assessments for collecting the School Rate was next taken up. It appeared that he had collected the School Rate for the years 1873 and 1874 and had got no remuneration for doing so, the Board having neglected to make any arrangement at the proper time. Mr Peter proposed that the remuneration should be three pounds for each collection of the Rate. Mr Low proposed that the payments for the years 1873–74 should be withdrawn and that the remuneration should be £2 per annum. The Collector said that rather than do that, he would give up the post reserving his claim for payment of the collections of the years 1873 & 74; and the meeting abruptly terminated.'

At the following meeting on 7th June 1875, a vote was taken as to whether or not extra money should be paid to the Collector for collecting the School Rate. It was decided that no remuneration should be given, whereupon Mr Proctor intimated his resignation.

There is no record in the Kirk Session Minutes of the appointment of George Proctor as Session Clerk, but the Minute of November 7th 1858 records his resignation. George Andrew, the local blacksmith was appointed in his place. Mr Proctor was re-elected on December 7th 1862 following George Andrew's death, and was to hold the post until his own death. Mr Proctor preached on average twice a year from the pulpit of Kemnay, he being a probationer preacher.

The advent of compulsory education in 1872 no doubt made considerable changes to the life of George Proctor. Since his arrival in Kemnay in 1857 he had been his own master and had been teaching those children who came to school seeking to better themselves through the medium of education. Now, however, it was decreed that all children between the ages of five and thirteen years of age must attend school. This in itself would have meant a large increase in the roll, and no doubt a number of these would have been reluctant scholars. Add to this the fact that George Proctor was no longer his own boss but an employee of the School Board. Needless to say, he did not always accept his new situation with good grace, and quite often we find he is at loggerheads with the School Board. More often than not the problem was money.

One of the first tasks of the newly elected School Board was to extend the school buildings. This they did by erecting a completely new building which was to act as a female and infant school, the teacher of which was Miss Webster, very capable and highly regarded. It should be noted, however, that she was a younger woman, reasonably fresh from college and not set in her ways. Her relationship with the School Board was cordial and the Inspector's report on her department of the school was very good.

On the other hand, in November 1874 we find George Proctor lodging a claim against the School Board for £6 for an iron railing which he had taken over at valuation when he came to the school some seventeen years previously. This the Board did not accept.

Towards the end of 1875 the School Board, following complaints from Mr Proctor of overcrowding in his department, asked that he discuss with Miss Webster the moving of all the girls and infants to the new school. Miss Webster's entry in the log book states that she had had no communication from Mr Proctor, whereas the entry in Mr Proctor's log says that: 'Most of the children asked to go to the other school have not gone, their parents holding that they have the right to send their children where they please.'

The problem again arose towards the end of 1876, when a deputation from the Board was appointed to call on Mr Proctor and arrange to have the pupils transferred. Mr Proctor's log entry for November 3rd 1876 reads: 'The School Board have signified their willingness that pupils preparing for the First Standard and under be sent over to the Female School, and that none should be admitted into this school who are not fit to enter the class preparing for passing in the Second Standard. This will be a great relief. This arrangement to take effect in the beginning of next week.'

Fuller entries are found in the log book of the Female School.

> October 20 1876. ...Sent for by Chairman of School Board, who stated that being too many in Boy's School the teacher wants relief; and he would now consent to send the boys of first Standard and all the girls to the Girls School. In reply stated that I had previously consented to do the very same thing, and that it was rather superfluous to create about it now. But that matters might be got smoothed took no further notice than intimate my willingness to do so provided the boys did not exceed 7 years of age.
>
> October 27. Another consultation with Chairman of the Schoolboard anent boys over 9. The Master states that there will be no difficulty with any but two boys whom I desire he should keep, and one girl. Two girls he says will not consent to come. These two I leave to his honour to send. Children to be sent on Tuesday 7th November.
>
> November 10. Boys sent according to arrangement. In the first place 5 boys very much over age. One of these does not know the letters of the alphabet, can make neither letters or figures. One is imbecile, while the other two have been badly neglected and can neither add nor subtract, can make the figures and letters but that is all. Of the whole lot, not one could pass Standard 1st Arithmetic. One might pass in writing, and probably eight or ten in reading. What is to be done in the case is rather perplexing, and shows pretty clearly why the Master should have ignored the Minute of December 1875, and make a show of treating anew as if such a Minute did not exist. Had they been sent in even March 1876, something might have been done for them, but now a bare pass is above what can be hoped for. Two girls left to the Master's honour have not put in appearance.

One can be sympathetic with Miss Webster's concern when it is realised that the grant earned by the school depended on the standard of the pupils at the annual inspection in February. Some of this grant was payable to the teacher as part of her salary. A lot of extra work was put in to try and bring the children up to some reasonable standard by that time.

May 16 1877. The following is summary of Inspector's Report. After the examination in February and from the unfair way in which this department has been treated during the year, it is only fair to inscribe the report of Boys Department. At the same time it is to be hoped that the injudicious meddling in school matters therein referred to will not be repeated to obstruct the work of the present year. As all changes that absolutely can be avoided are to be deeply deplored from the pernicious effects both on discipline and education.

Mr Proctor's department: The attendance here is reduced by the transference lately of about 40 of the worst qualified pupils to the female department. The pass in Standard subjects is very good, a little below that of last year, but would have been considerably lower had not the transference been made. Writing both on copies and slates is good, but the copies regularly in use should be shewn. The meanings of words are given regularly and grammar is ahead of requirements. The pupil teacher has made most satisfactory progress during the year both in his paper and teaching…

Miss Webster's department: This department continues to be taught with much fidelity. That the pass is not so good as last year is due partly to the teachers being for some time in poor health, but mainly to the transference of about forty pupils from the male department in the end of 1876. This transference ought to have been made much earlier or not till the Inspection is over. Of the twenty five failures in the first Standard, nineteen are made by pupils thus transferred for which Miss Webster is not responsible.

Besides such an importation of fresh pupils so shortly before the inspection must have acted as a serious drag on the general instruction. The division of labour is very unequal, there being only seventy eight present in the male department and a hundred and thirty nine in the female department, with two pupil teachers. The intelligence and grammar of the second and third standards are very fair but would appear to better advantage if the answering were more distinct. Arithmetic of the fourth and fifth standards is weak. A creditable appearance was made in Geography and

History. The Grammar of the fourth and fifth standards requires attention. The infants are well managed, very good singing and industrial work. I am quite satisfied with the teacher's fidelity, and have no doubt about the continued efficiency of the teacher's instruction when the school shall have recovered from the late untimely influx. A Middleton, B J Milne and M F MacDonald have passed well.

Signed A. C.

By the time of the next Inspector's report, Miss Webster had taken up a post at Commerce Street School in Aberdeen. The new Headmistress of the Female School was Miss Annie Don and the other staff were Miss Agnes Darling, teacher; Barbara J Milne, pupil teacher (P.T.) in 5th year; Marjory F McDonald, P.T. in 4th year, Elizabeth Herd, P.T. in 1st year. The report shows the school in far better light than in the previous year. There was one detracting comment in the whole report; 'the only noteworthy failure being in the first Standard, many of whom are just seven years of age.' The report finishes with: 'I am to state that B J Milne having been placed in the first class in the Midsummer Examination 1877 for Queen's Scholarships is considered to have passed well the Examination required by article 70(e), and is therefore qualified to bring a grant at the rate of sixty shillings under article 19(e) to the school for the part of the year during which she served there.'

The school work carries on and it is sometimes difficult to follow the happenings as the log entries do not always tie up. An interesting entry by Mr Proctor on April 2nd 1880 reads: 'Gave out Monday and Tuesday of next week as holidays. This is the last day in the Old Parish School for myself and the Higher Standards. Commence work in the New Schoolroom on Wednesday next.' No word of the move is contained in the log book of the Girls Department but the move does not seem to have gone altogether smoothly as there is correspondence between Mr Proctor and the School Board to the effect that the female teachers have not acted according to his instructions.

The log book of the Girls Department ceases in 1882 with no reason being given. It is to be assumed that the two schools were then amalgamated and run as one unit. From then on little can be gleaned from Mr Proctor's entries other than staff movements and the like.

The entry of June 10th 1892 records that Mr Edward Alexander M.A. son of the Station Agent at Monymusk was elected assistant on Wednesday. This might seem to be a rather insignificant entry, but it helps to date and explain the school photograph of that era (p47). The identity of the two teachers can now be ascertained with little doubt; the bearded gentleman being Mr Proctor and the other Mr Alexander. The previous log entry mentioning the move from the Old Parish School explains why the photo was taken at the new school. It also gives a date of between June 1892 and July 1894.

The entry of July 25th 1894 reads simply: 'Gave out the summer holidays to-day at one o'clock.' Thus ended George Proctor's headmastership of thirty seven years at Kemnay School.

That the School Board members found working with Mr Proctor very difficult comes out very clearly in their Minutes. As early as 1883 it is proposed that a retiring allowance be made to him. This motion was asked to be left lying on the table.

The following is part of a letter from W Kendall Burnett to the Scottish Education Department:

> 'I return enclosed the form therein referred to duly completed and have now to explain the reason why our Board have been unable to answer question 13 page 4 in the affirmative*. Mr Proctor being an ex Parochial Teacher assumes that he has rights which the Board are of opinion he has not or should not have and he has endeavoured in every way possible to thwart the Board in the arrangements made by them for the working of the school and has moreover on several occasions made arrangements of his own in opposition to the wishes of the Board. The Board consider that by inserting the 'Yes' they would be placing themselves in a somewhat anomalous position in regard to the matter referred to; and while they have no dissatisfaction to express in regard to his moral character they feel that My Lords should thus be made awair (sic) in regard to the differences which exist in regard to the conducting of the work.'

* Question 13 asked 'Are the managers satisfied with the teacher's character, conduct and attention to duty during the past year?'

Kemnay School circa 1893

The bearded gentleman is the Rev. George Proctor and the other teacher Mr Edward Alexander

Discussions between the Board and Mr Proctor regarding a retiring allowance started in 1892, but it was not until May 1894 that final terms were agreed. One might say that Mr Proctor had the last word, in that he requested use of the Schoolhouse until Whitsunday 1895.

Mr Proctor built 'The Evergreens' for his retirement. It was a superior house in the Terrace which, from the middle of this century has been known as Birkenshaw. Sadly he did not live long to enjoy his retirement. He died on 20th October 1898. His wife Isabella Cheyne, who he married in the early 1870's lived until 1911. In the 1871 census her father, with whom she was staying, is recorded as a superannuated teacher aged sixty nine and staying at Kemnay Cottage. This was the site of the private school run by the laird, A G Burnett.

The school log of Oct. 21st 1898 records the following:

> 'The Rev George Proctor M.A. who for the long period of forty years was headmaster of this School died at Kemnay on the 20th inst. following a short illness at the age of 68. The funeral takes place on Monday the 24th inst. and so school will be closed that day. It may be noted that Mr Proctor retired some four years ago.'

The School Board Minute of 2nd November 1898 records:

> 'It was resolved that the following minute of sympathy on the death of Mr Proctor late Schoolmaster should be sent to his widow and the clerk instructed accordingly. 'The School Board desire to record their sense of the great loss the Parish of Kemnay has sustained in the death of Rev Geo. Proctor M.A, whose life was devoted to the interests of education in Kemnay and who occupied the position of Headmaster in the Kemnay Parish School for the very long period of thirty seven years. They desire further to express their sincere sympathy with his widow in her bereavement.'

At the Kirk Session meeting of 11th November 1898, the following minute was adopted with reference to the late Rev. Geo. Proctor, who died on the 20th October last, and a copy was ordered to be sent to his widow:

> 'The Kirk Session desire to express their great regret at the loss by death of their esteemed clerk, the Rev George Proctor M.A.

His services were highly valued by them, and his presence in the court was always helpful. They feel they have lost a good friend as well as a trusted officebearer. They desire to express their sincerest sympathy with his widow in her great bereavement.'

William Alexander

By 1893 Compulsory Education had been on the go for some twenty years and we find an interest now being shown in Secondary Education. The School Board was unsure of the demand locally but they were very enthusiastic in putting forward the name of Kemnay School as a centre. It was also noted that there were about sixteen pupils travelling daily to Aberdeen for Secondary Education.

Following protracted negotiations, Mr Proctor finally agreed to retire in the summer of 1894. His successor was Mr William Alexander from Aberchirder, who was elected from an application list of thirty four. He came to the school at a time of considerable upheaval. Building works were in progress to enlarge the school. There were insufficient staff and overcrowding was a further problem. The latter was settled by moving a class to the Public Hall for the duration of the building works. A temporary teacher was also appointed.

An inspection of the new buildings was made by the Secondary Education Committee in view of the establishment of a Secondary Department. It was to be recommended to give a grant of £100 towards the new buildings. The relationship between the new headmaster and the School Board was completely different to that which had existed previously. More consultation was made and it seemed as though new life had been breathed into the school. The curriculum was extended with the introduction of Classics. In 1895 we find that Neil Meldrum gained the first bursary for the Garioch District.

The report of the annual inspection in February 1897 gives the roll as consisting of 202 boys, 192 girls, a total of 394. The teaching staff consisted of: Mr W Alexander, Certificated; Mr Edward Alexander, assistant teacher (they were both M.A. of Aberdeen University); Miss Ellen Scott, probationer 1st year; Miss Sophie Yeats, probationer 2nd year; Miss Margaret Anderson, probationer 2nd year; Miss Jane Emslie, assistant teacher; Christina Hardie, pupil teacher 3rd year.

At that time there were only seven rooms in the school. One can easily imagine the difficulties that could be encountered by staff, some of whom were little more than schoolchildren themselves. In 1897 also, Kemnay along with Huntly were the only two schools in Aberdeenshire to receive maximum grant under the Dick Bequest Scheme.

It may be thought that in-service training is an innovation of the recent past. In 1897 we find that the 'Headmaster was away at examination in connection with science and art department.' Again in 1901 'the Headmaster has been elected by the County Council to a Modern Language Scholarship of £30, he is to study in France for two months.'

Standards rose in the school, and it was not long before former pupils were making their mark in further education. A milestone was reached in 1901 when the scholars were granted a half holiday in honour of...

> 'Netta Terras Gordon, who has received the whole of her education at this school stands First in the published list of the successful candidates at the Aberdeen Bursary Competition.'

This talented young lady, daughter of Alexander Gordon a local general merchant, went on to study at Aberdeen University where she graduated M.A. in 1905 with First Class honours in Classics. She was also awarded the Simpson Greek Prize of £65, the Seafield Gold Medal for Latin, the silver pen for Greek and the Geddes Memorial Prize for the same subject. She took up a teaching post at St. Columba's Girls School, Kilmalcolm before emigrating to Canada in 1908 to become head of the Classics Department at Havergill College in Toronto. She died in September 1993 at the age of 108 years.

It was a rare occasion when pupils from the school did not appear in the list of successful candidates at Aberdeen University Bursary Competition. Many pupils benefitted from County Council Bursaries and also received help by way of other Bequest Funds. Over the years many pupils went on to further education at centres throughout the country and produced results that were noted with great pride in the pages of the school log.

Several of the teachers gained promotion from the school. On February 28th 1897, 'Mr Edward Alexander M.A. who has been assistant in the senior department of this school for nearly seven years was presented with a massive marble time piece in recognition of his services. He begins work on Monday as Headmaster of Keig Public School.'

Further changes to the education system were on the horizon. In 1905 a

Higher Grade Department was recognised at the school, and soon the School Board had plans afoot to extend the school to cope with the extra pupils and subjects taught. This new department was to cater for pupils all the way up Donside, many of whom stayed in the village during the week and travelled home only at weekends. Those from Alford and nearer travelled daily by train. It was not until 1927 that senior education started at Alford.

The greatly extended school was opened for use in October 1906, and this extension was to satisfy the needs of the school, albeit cramped at times, until after the Second World War when the school kitchen, dining hall and technical hut were erected.

Mr Alexander was a tall, erect gentleman with a small goatee beard. A stern disciplinarian, he was fair in his dealings towards children. On one occasion, aware that the apples in his garden were disappearing, he asked some of the older boys to keep a lookout on his fruit trees one lunch time. The reported boys were duly asked to report to his private room at a stated time. The culprits were lined up and given a lecture. They were then asked to hand in a penny to his office. He was well aware that if word got to the parents about what had happened, then a thrashing was in store for the miscreants. At the end of the week, they were once more lined up and all received their pennies back.

On another occasion during springtime when rodden whistles, the small instruments immortalised by Hamewith were all the rage, one lad had made a particularly piercing whistle, and was deeving everybody with the noise. Word of this came to the headmaster's ears and he stood the culprit in front of the class and asked all about his masterpiece. Following the description and history of it, he said to the boy, 'Let me hear you play it.' This the boy did, and he was all the more encouraged by Mr Alexander who would not let him stop until he was well and truly out of puff.

Similarly, a boy who had been absent from school for some time was questioned in the Head's private room regarding his persistent truancy. The boy reported that he was somewhat downhearted at being continually kept back in his class. Mr Alexander set him a test on his school work which he passed creditably. He was then handed a sixpence and was told to stick into his learning. This ended his truancy and he progressed favourably following the incident.

There were many trying times during his headmastership. Overcrowding, coupled with shortage of teaching staff were recurrent problems. During the First World War, feelings ran high when word came back of those former pupils, some still in their teens, who were killed in active service for their country. One such entry towards the end of 1916 containing the names of four young men is followed by 'many have been murdered' but 'murdered' has later been erased and 'killed' inserted above. Marianus Cumming, who joined the teaching staff in September 1913 was called up immediately on outbreak of hostilities, he being a member of the Territorial Forces.

In June 1915, the following entry appears in the log book:

> 'Intimation has just been received that Marianus A Cumming M.A. teacher of the Supplementary class who has been in France and Belgium with the Gordon Highlanders since the 'U' Company crossed to the continent, has been killed by a sniper. His loss is deeply felt and we mourn in great sorrow for one who by his fine life and noble death will be held by all of us in everlasting honour.'

Throughout the duration of the Great War, there are listed eighteen names of former pupils and staff who had been killed on the field of battle. It must have been a considerable heartbreak to the headmaster to record the untimely deaths of so many of the cream of his former pupils. It would no doubt have been with pride that entry in the log book was made of those who had gained commissions in the forces or whose actions gained them medals.

The pupils also played their part as can be seen by the entry of November 5th 1915:
> 'The girls of the school have just finished a large number of woollen comforters, socks, mitts, helmets &c., for the men of the fleet and the soldiers.'

Much of the testing of the school and pupils was done by visiting inspectors. Various inspectors called, each examining in his own specific subjects. The results of these examinations influenced the children's academic progress, and more importantly, the amount of grant the school received from the different educational trusts and bodies. Little wonder that at one time there was a great effort, prior to the annual inspection, to cram knowledge into the heads of the pupils. Sometimes the questions and answers would be passed from school to school in advance of the inspector's visit.

A report was sent annually to the school from the inspector giving details of his visit to the school, starting with a general resumé of the school in general before describing the standards found in each of the individual subjects taught, which included English, Latin, Greek, French, Maths, Experimental Science, Drawing, Sewing, Singing, Manual Instruction, Physical Exercises. The School Report of September 1923 gave a very good assessment of the teaching achievement and pupil standard for the final year of Mr Alexander's Headmastership. English, Classics, Mathematics, Modern Languages, Science and Drawing all revealed that teaching was in competent hands; instruction was being carried out with great vigour and skill, with Science singled out as a course having teaching of exceptional merit.

In this particular report, reference was made to Mr Alexander:

> 'In his conduct of the School, he has shown sound judgment, unflagging energy and an unfailing sense of duty. He leaves behind him a School which is efficient in all branches of instruction and a personal record of the most exemplary and devoted service'.

One example of the level of achievement in the school is noted in October 1922, when Thomas Paterson became first Bursar at the Divinity Hall, Edinburgh with a Bursary value of £97 and in November he gained a top prize in a competition open to Scotland for those studying Divinity at Edinburgh. He later became a Minister. In June, 1923, Florence J. Malcolm and Bernard MacDonald both graduated M.B., Ch.B from Aberdeen University. These achievements alone mirror some of the abilities of the pupils of previous years, and they were joined by many more in the time of Mr Robertson's Headmastership.

In the second decade of the twentieth century, the school roll averaged 450 with around eighty in the higher grade or secondary department. Over the years, there were considerable changes in the teaching staff. Most contracts of engagement were on two months notice either way. Seldom did a teacher work out the required notice. Sometimes a substitute was offered by the teacher wishing to leave, quite often not. Many teachers gave sterling service to the school, often over a period of many years.

John Minto Robertson

John Minto Robertson, M.A., LL.D., F.E.I.S. was Headmaster of Kemnay Secondary school from August 1923 until June 1948 – twenty five years of distinguished service. He came to Kemnay from Turriff Secondary school, where he had held the post of Classical Master, and he inherited an outstanding level of teacher ability and pupil attainment.

On his arrival at Kemnay, thirty two new pupils enrolled in the Higher Grade from outside schools – a record enrolment for the school, with 74 pupils in the first year of that Grade. There were, in fact, 134 pupils in the Higher Grade – the greatest number by far in the history of the school and the whole work was carried out by five teachers, one of whom was the Headmaster himself. The school had been understaffed in the past and now, with these additional pupils and classes at either end 'there is a claimant demand for two more Assistants ' (so reads the school Report).

From these early days, Mr Robertson drew his staff together and put forward new ideas – Football for boys, Hockey or Basketball for Girls; the possibility of a Literary and Debating Society for Senior classes on a Friday afternoon during winter; the question of Boy Scouts and Girl Guides and the need for a Sale of Work at some date in the future to raise funds to support these school activities. He sincerely felt that pupils should have a broader view of life rather than simply lessons.

The staff were in sympathy with the various ideas and it was agreed to call meetings of Higher Grade boys and girls respectively, to set before them the various schemes, hear their own opinions and, if well received, proceed to elect officials and take the necessary steps to raise money, get the suitable paraphernalia, playing fields or pitches and so forth. The very next day, the ideas were put to the pupils. They met and elected their own office-bearers – the boys to take up football and the girls net or basketball.

This movement forward was surely a very democratic way of bringing new interests into the lives of the pupils and, with the involvement of some teachers also, to bring a feeling of togetherness within the school and community .

In January 1924, the "Soup Experiment" began. With gifts of vegetables and potatoes etc., the soup was made in large pots, but later a boiler was procured for this purpose. From then until 3rd April, a total of 4,948 plates of hot soup were served, over 53 school days, at an average of 93.3 per day. The highest number on any one day was 127. A large copper boiler was then recommended for the following year. The price paid by the pupils was one penny for a plate of soup. For those travelling a long distance to school, either on foot, by bicycle, bus or train, the hot soup at 'dinner-time', must have been most nourishing and satisfying. Many pupils came from Alford or further up country – Tillyfourie, Cluny, Monymusk, Tough, Blairdaff, Fetternear as well as all the country areas nearer Kemnay. The "Soup Experiment" was a real success, continuing until a canteen started in 1948.

A step forward also was the arrival of a new Cyclostyle from the Education Authority – this was real progress! Special mention must also be made of an acquisition in that same year which meant that the main Hall was enhanced by the addition of a large bookcase. This was purchased for the school from the 'Activities' Fund, at the Rev. Andrew Downie's Roup (Minister of Kemnay Parish Church) and immediately well filled with volumes, also purchased at the Roup and from Bisset's Bookshop in Aberdeen. A bookcase, belonging to the Education Authority, was also transferred to the Hall and it is reported "that the Hall is beginning to look really a place of beauty". These bookcases remained, full of the books, right through Mr Robertson's time and beyond, but sadly, in later years, mysteriously disappeared. Still in the same year – 1924 – the school had the afternoon off on the occasion of the induction of the Rev. Robert Keltie, M.A. to the vacant charge in the Parish of Kemnay (Church of Scotland).

In June, thirteen boys attended the first class in Scouting (at 8 a.m.!) and were under instruction from the Headmaster. At the end of the next week, the pupils were ready to pass Tenderfoot tests. A very significant event took place on the 24th June – the first of the Open Air performances was given by pupils of Scenes and Songs from Shakespeare, with Old English dances, in the policies of Kemnay House. Mr John A. Burnett of Kemnay House presided at both afternoon and evening performances which were a great success. The money raised (£26 4s) went to help start the fund for the Kemnay Boy Scouts and Girl Guides.

This was the forerunner of annual performances – in later years, entire plays were presented, right up to the time of Mr Robertson's retiral. All of the performances were staged under a very old, enormous beech tree at

Kemnay House still standing in this last decade of the twentieth century. Very many pupils over the years were involved in these performances and numerous pictures of the early days were hung in the small Hall at the school. In later years, these disappeared. The same fate seems to have befallen the very large frames which hung in the main Hall, with a variety of pictures of each separate play produced. Those who did take part in the plays still have some pictures of those early days.

There was much criticism from some quarters that only certain, favoured pupils were chosen for parts, spoken or unspoken and that much school teaching time was taken up in rehearsing. However, those chosen had to show the ability to memorise, to speak clearly and to act as directed. All rehearsals took place after school hours or in the evenings, mostly out of doors and it was only during the last week when any school time was used, for rehearsal at Kemnay House or on the lawn of the schoolhouse. It was quite unbelievable that, in the Literature Paper of the Higher Leaving Certificate Examination of 1945, one of the questions asked was what were the advantages of performing Shakespeare Plays in the open air. This was a real gift for those pupils sitting the examination that year.

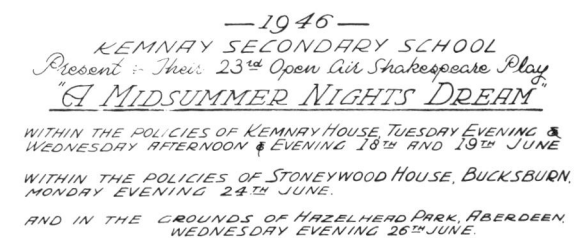

— 1946 —
KEMNAY SECONDARY SCHOOL
Present :- Their 23rd Open Air Shakespeare Play
"A MIDSUMMER NIGHTS DREAM"

WITHIN THE POLICIES OF KEMNAY HOUSE, TUESDAY EVENING & WEDNESDAY AFTERNOON & EVENING 18th AND 19th JUNE

WITHIN THE POLICIES OF STONEYWOOD HOUSE, BUCKSBURN, MONDAY EVENING 24th JUNE.

AND IN THE GROUNDS OF HAZELHEAD PARK, ABERDEEN, WEDNESDAY EVENING 26th JUNE.

Caption from the framed Shakespeare play photographs of 1946

As the years went by, the plays became very popular and people came from long distances to see them performed. Mr Robertson was very musical himself and always chose excellent background music. For some years a number of talented musicians came from Aberdeen to help and the singing of the Shakespearean songs by pupils was excellent. The costumes for the various plays came from Helena Thom in Aberdeen and latterly from Bambers in Glasgow. For his work in this sphere, Mr Robertson received an LL.D. Honorary Degree from Aberdeen University on 28th June 1945. From then on he was always referred to as Dr. Robertson.

The Cast from Shakespeare's play 'A Winter's Tale'

Back Row: Chrissie Dunn, Leochel Cushnie, Margaret Duncan, Alice Nicol, Georgina Gordon, Mary Skene, Betty Dickson, Agnes Morgan, Annie Harper, Enid Robb. 3rd Row: Arthur Paterson, *Name Unknown*, Jean McHardy, Blanche Daun, Walter Gilbert, John Sim, Charlie Brown, Grace McWilliam, Sheila Paterson, Gordon Ingram. 2nd Row: Margaret Milne, Violet Birnie, Margaret Robertson, Jimmy Morgan, Jean Edwards, Nancy Roger, Maria Thom, Ethel Connon. Front Row: Sybil Moir and Ella Gall

The 1927 Cast from Shakespeare's play 'Much Ado About Nothing'

Janet MacNicol, Mary Robertson, Margaret Robertson, Violet Laing, *Name Unknown*, Alex Williams, Frances Gray, Alice Buchan, Lily McLean, Lesley Buchan, Nicholas Forbes, Front Row: Annie Paterson and Mary McLennan

Outwith the school activities, J. Minto Robertson played an important role in village life. In May 1924 a public meeting was held to inaugurate a local troop of Boy Scouts. Mr Robertson agreed to act as Scoutmaster, Mr John Burnett was elected President with the Rev. R. Keltie as Vice President. The Headmaster was also Chairman and Mr John R. Gall, Secretary, pro tem. In June, the school had another afternoon free for the opening of the new Kemnay Tennis Courts, which were fully used over many years and continue to be a lively centre of activity.

When school resumed in August after the summer holidays, there were 153 pupils in the Higher Grade but still the same number of staff to cope. It was necessary, because of the number in the second year Higher Grade – 56 – to break the class into 'A' and 'B' categories. The 'A' pupils normally studied languages, mathematics, science and the 'B' pupils preferred woodwork, sewing, cooking, art. This highlighted the need for further teaching staff but, despite Mr Robertson's strenuous efforts, the Director of Education could not supply an interim teacher. On the Director's suggestion, Mr Robertson then wrote directly to the Chairman of the Authority and the Chairman of the Staffing Committee asking for an interim.

Nothing happened for a week to relieve the situation which "was almost intolerable". However, help came the following week with the arrival of Mr Peter R. Roy and Mr Charles McPherson, two graduates who had been pupils at Kemnay, and they had, in preparation for their attendance at the Training Centre, to do practice in teaching. They were both therefore utilised in the class crisis. After further representations to the authorities, Miss I.D.Blake, M.A. was offered as an interim and as a student in training. She, therefore, arrived to assist in French, English and Latin, and, with some other reorganisation, involving teachers in the Primary school, the situation was slightly eased. As the Headmaster himself did not have the authority to make some of these changes, he found it necessary to remind the Inspector, Mr Crawford, to make the necessary suggestions to the Authority.

On top of this turmoil, the Headmaster was responsible for overseeing the compilation of timetables for the Higher Grade and this was a great strain on him after the start of the session. The Report states "the strain would have been obviated if the Director had granted the perfectly reasonable request made to him before the holidays ended, of an interim teacher".

The years roll on with the Inspector's Reports – some excellent results, some not so good – depending on pupils and teachers too, but one comment is notable – "Admirable spirit and enterprise have been shown in raising funds for a library of suitable books for the use of each class." Armistice Day came around in November and in 1924 the ceremony was observed by the school at 11 a.m. A service was held with local Ministers officiating and the youngest pupil laid a wreath at the school War Memorial. This service was repeated each year, on Armistice Day, during Mr Robertson's time as Headmaster.

In February 1925, the Girl Guides were inaugurated under their Captain Miss Annie Watt. The company had a membership of thirty. At that time also, the Headmaster began early morning sessions for Leaving Certificate pupils in Latin, at 7.45 a.m. Still in February of that year, the Boy Scouts started to meet in the Manse barn which was to be their first Headquarters. Numbers attending school continued to rise and in April, with the intake of infants, the number of scholars rose to – Primary 212, Remove 26 and Secondary 122 – a total of 360. The class called Remove covered those pupils who had finished primary at Easter but did not join the secondary school until August. During their three months or thereby in Remove, they were able to have a little taste of all the subjects available in the Higher Grade.

At this time in the school, there was lack of proper accommodation and it was agreed that some alterations be made in the Primary classrooms. The boys of the Woodwork class planted potatoes in the school garden to help out with the Hot Dinners for the next winter and the Boy Scouts worked on for an hour after school closed at 4.15 p.m. to help get the potato crop harvested.

Another first at Kemnay was the setting up of a North East War Savings Association Branch in the school – each teacher looking after his or her class with one teacher acting as Treasurer for the whole. The total contributed in the first week was £11 16s 1d. This was a very auspicious start.

In June of that year, two pupils were given certificates for perfect attendance – special mention was made of Fred Mitchell, who had completed six years perfect attendance and Wm.Glennie who had completed 9½ years perfect attendance – the entire time he had been at school. These were special prizes from the Activities Fund.

Kemnay Girl Guides

Back Row: Nell Donald, Bunty Forbes, Eva Taylor, Jean Edwards, Ethel Lawson, *Name Unknown*, Ella Gall, Nellie Bremner, Ethel Scott, Mary Taylor. Middle Row: Bunty Moir, Sheila Stephen, Vera King, Bet Petrie, Dora Cruickshank, Miss Innes, *Name Unknown*, Isobel Morgan, Agnes Davidson, Dora Law, *Name Unknown*, Isobel Diack. Front Row: Agnes Beaton, Grace McWilliam, Margaret Wood, Mary Harvey, Blanche Daun, Sheila Paterson, *Name Unknown*, *Name Unknown*, Hilda Walker, Margaret Duncan, Maisie Moir and Flora Cruickshank

Kemnay Scouts

Left to Right: J. Minto Robertson, Fred Mitchell, The Laird, Davie Gordon, Bill Gray, *Name Unknown*, Bertie Downie, Doug Henderson, *Name Unknown*, *Name Unknown*, Archie Nicol, *Name Unknown*, *Name Unknown*, Bill Duncan, Leslie Mitchell, Albert Hunter Diack, *Name Unknown* and Tom Robertson.

Along with his other duties, the Headmaster was taking the whole of the singing for the Higher Grade. In the autumn, the idea of starting a school Magazine was mooted, and a meeting of the Secondary school was held after prayers in the afternoon to discuss this. Accordingly a small committee of pupils was formed, with Hunter Diack and Annie Laing as Joint Editors. The English Department was to exercise some friendly supervision and it was hoped the first issue would be ready for Christmas. When the magazine did come out, it was printed by W. & W. Lindsay, 28 Market Street, Aberdeen and cost one shilling. There was a wealth of reading contained in one of the first copies, dated December 1926. A resumé of the activities within the school, articles from pupils who had been abroad or gone abroad to stay; articles on different areas of the countryside; poetry and small illustrations relating to the articles and many advertisements from local businessmen and farther afield – A. Henry and Son, Bakers; J. & W. Morgan, Boots and Shoes; John Barron, Butcher; Wishart, Jamieson & Ewen, General Merchants, Monymusk; William Gerrard, Butcher; Mr G. Cruickshank, photographer; Albert Findlater, Cycle and Motor Engineer; Wm. Bremner, Watchmaker; Alexander Gordon & Son, General Merchants; R. Reid & Son, Shoemakers; John. A.Taylor, Outfitter/Hairdresser, etc.; P. Strachan & Son, Grocers/Drapers, Ironmongers; W.G. Macfarquhar, Chemist; John Pirie & Son, Car Hire; Cecilia M. Bremner, Teacher of Music; Alex. S. Weir, Chemist; Andrew Petrie & Sons, Drapery/Millinery/ Groceries, etc.; M. McLeay, Baker; Alex. Sangster, Outfitter; James H.Stewart, Baker, Alford; James Curr, Bridge of Alford; Falconers, Aberdeen; C.Bruce Miller & Co., Pianos, organs, music, etc.; The Rubber Shop; Henderson Brothers, for Football Jerseys, etc. and Hutchisons, Saddlers; Alex. Scott & Co., plus Burnett's Classes and The Gregg schools, where many pupils learned to be good shorthand writers and typists. A wealth of detail all for one shilling!

The report of H.M.'s Inspector for August 1925, expressed some very gratifying comments, firstly on the Primary Department, now with a total roll of 220.

> "As the staff consists of five teachers, covering seven classes, the organisation for teaching purposes is necessarily abnormal. Despite this difficulty, however, the discipline is excellent and the results of instruction are highly creditable. The teachers are to be congratulated, not merely on the proficiency of their classes, but

also on the general air of neatness, tidiness and politeness which pervades them."

The Report for the Higher Grade classes speaks of:

"...good work in the English Department, conscientious and creditable progress in Mathematics, satisfactory presentations in Latin, skilful teaching in modern languages with a satisfactory standard of attainment; the work in Science is sound with pupils being self-reliant and intelligent and the teaching of a stimulating character. Instruction in Art is highly meritorious, reflecting great credit on the teacher. Music has received a lot of attention with considerable effort being made to carry out a full programme of work. More time per scholar is needed and also a finer grading so that the subject can have a secure, progressive study. Excellent choral pieces have been selected and delightfully rendered. Solos and quartets of high quality serve to diversify the instruction. The tests for sight-singing both from staff and solfa notations are creditable and surprising accuracy of ear is shown."

Kemnay Secondary school had, over many years, particularly in Mr Robertson's time, a great reputation for singing and music. He, himself, was an excellent bass/baritone singer and gave leadership in this. Many concerts were produced involving each class in the school, and these were always a sell-out with excellent acting and singing.

An interesting entry in the school log book records that, in October 1925, a party of 53 went to HM Theatre, Aberdeen, in the evening, to see a performance of Macbeth, produced by Henry Baynton. This would have been the first of many such visits which continued into the forties, when a season of plays was performed annually, under the direction of the Shakespearean actor, Donald Wolfit, and very many pupils went to see them, sometimes travelling by train from Kemnay. Mr Robertson, in fact, after that first Theatre visit, was invited to the Training Centre, in Aberdeen, by Miss Grainger Stewart, to meet Mr Baynton, who was being entertained by the Women's Shakespeare Society.

Morning Prayers for Higher Grade and half the Primary school were held in the main hall with Miss Jeannie Bremner, Infant Mistress, playing the organ. In later years, John Morgan taught the violin and as a result, an excellent orchestra came into being, which took part in many concerts, church services and the like. John Morgan was a first class musician, singer and composer, who later became Choirmaster at the Parish Church.

Another evening out for Higher Grade pupils was in March 1926, when the Headmaster took a party of 43 to HM Theatre to see Sir F. R. Benson in 'She Stoops to Conquer'. The party travelled by Jaffray's two motor buses and a small car. In May 1926, the country was affected by the General Strike and, as a result, no trains were moving. Some of the pupils managed to get to school by bus and "the train pupils have made exemplary attendance". Some cycled the twenty odd miles to school, and for many, it meant leaving home before 7 a.m. and not reaching home again until 8 p.m. or later.

At the end of that month, Miss Jeannie Bremner took a party of 27 children to the Aberdeen Music Festival, to enter in an 'Action Song' and 'Singing Game' Competition. Two other teachers went along to help and Second Place was gained with the 'Action Song'. The children then had tea in Findlay's Dairy and went to the Picture House cinema for two hours. They travelled by bus and got home at 8 p.m. The expenses were met from the school Activities Fund and Miss Bremner gave the treat to the Pictures. Probably some of the children had never left Kemnay or been anywhere near Aberdeen before.

In June, the results of the Donaldson Trust Bible Examination were announced, with nine out of eleven candidates being successful. Kemnay had the first three places for 4th year students – Janet W. MacNicol (89%), Margaret Robertson (86%) and Alex. M. Kellock (83%). Amongst the 5th year students, Frances Gray was 2nd, Ishbel MacPherson 6th, Jessie McKenzie 7th and James F. Mitchell 8th, out of a total of 55 competitors. In the 6th year, the 1st prize went to Hunter Diack with 97%, the 2nd prize to Annie Laing with 92% and the third to Lizzie Marion Ewen with 91%. Out of the total of 148 competitors in Aberdeen City and County, Banff and Kincardine, Kemnay pupils won twenty guineas in total prize money. This was a magnificent achievement for Scripture Knowledge and over the following years there were several pupils from Kemnay in the Prize List right through to the mid-forties. Again further results came in 1926 by way of the Arts Bursary Competition with three candidates from the sixth year being placed.

In March 1927, an Adult Section of the Aberdeen County Library was opened in the school. There was a good issue of books and a further stock arrived making a total available of 222 volumes. This continued for many years, with different teachers and senior pupils being utilised to supervise the lending of books and their return.

A great day came in August 1927, when Mr Harry Green began duty as Singing Master. In later years, the Music Teacher was Mr Rogers and thereafter Miss Kate Johnston. Their duties were confined to the teaching of voice production, reading music and singing generally. They visited usually on a Thursday each week. The rest of the time class teachers took any singing, if they had that particular capability, and of course, the Headmaster himself.

In 1927 once again a very good report was given on all the subjects being taught at Kemnay Secondary school and the work of the teachers continued to be solid and methodical, with very conscientious oversight and guidance of pupils, from the very junior classes to the most senior.

In the main Hall of the school, there is a large Dux Board affixed to the

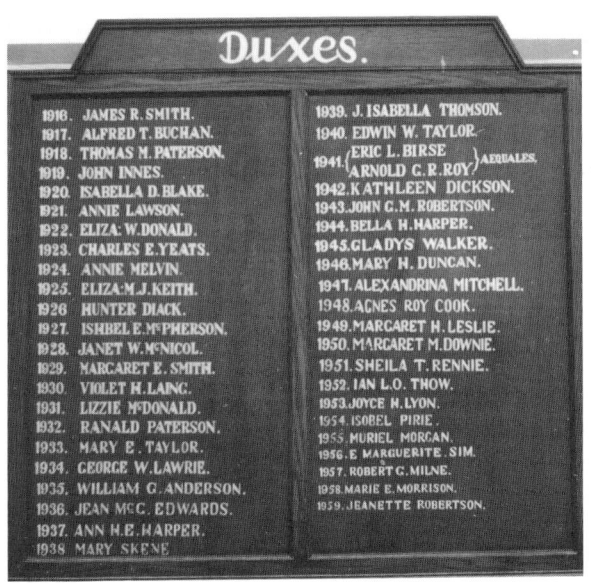

Duxes.

1916	JAMES R. SMITH.
1917	ALFRED T. BUCHAN.
1918	THOMAS M. PATERSON.
1919	JOHN INNES.
1920	ISABELLA D. BLAKE.
1921	ANNIE LAWSON.
1922	ELIZA: W. DONALD.
1923	CHARLES E. YEATS.
1924	ANNIE MELVIN.
1925	ELIZA: M.J. KEITH.
1926	HUNTER DIACK.
1927	ISHBEL E. McPHERSON.
1928	JANET W. McNICOL.
1929	MARGARET E. SMITH.
1930	VIOLET H. LAING.
1931	LIZZIE McDONALD.
1932	RANALD PATERSON.
1933	MARY E. TAYLOR.
1934	GEORGE W. LAWRIE.
1935	WILLIAM G. ANDERSON.
1936	JEAN McC. EDWARDS.
1937	ANN H.E. HARPER.
1938	MARY SKENE
1939	J. ISABELLA THOMSON.
1940	EDWIN W. TAYLOR.
1941	ERIC L. BIRSE / ARNOLD C.R. ROY } AEQUALES.
1942	KATHLEEN DICKSON.
1943	JOHN G.M. ROBERTSON.
1944	BELLA H. HARPER.
1945	GLADYS WALKER.
1946	MARY H. DUNCAN.
1947	ALEXANDRINA MITCHELL.
1948	AGNES ROY COOK.
1949	MARGARET H. LESLIE.
1950	MARGARET M. DOWNIE.
1951	SHEILA T. RENNIE.
1952	IAN L.O. THOW.
1953	JOYCE H. LYON.
1954	ISOBEL PIRIE.
1955	MURIEL MORGAN.
1956	E MARGUERITE. SIM.
1957	ROBERT G. MILNE.
1958	MARIE E. MORRISON.
1959	JEANETTE ROBERTSON.

wall presented by Mr A. S. Weir one of the village Pharmacists, recording the Duxes from the inception of prize-giving. However, no distinction was made when the Duxes were only Third year pupils when the school was down-graded in later years.

One item of note which Mr Robertson introduced to the school was a motto and badge. The motto – Disce Vivere – Learn How to Live – encompassed all that this man sought to instil in the minds of the pupils passing through the school. A badge was produced with a green background edged in fawn and with the letters K.S.S. written across, also in fawn. The motto was written, also in fawn, at the bottom. Many pupils had one of these sewn on their blazer jackets or on the front of the girls' gym tunics. Ties and scarves were also procured in the school colours.

Morning and afternoon prayers were well thought out with appropriate readings, prayers, hymns and psalms relevant to the events of the time – particularly during the years of the Second World War.

Many pupils will recall the word "Resurgam" which was learned and repeated every morning, following the fall of Poland. "We shall rise again" became part of the daily morning service, together with other patriotic phrases. The singing of the Lord's Prayer to the tune Langdon was much enjoyed, especially by those who could sing in harmony. During the war years, whilst Mr John Morgan, the Choirmaster was in the forces, Mr Robertson took on the task of keeping the choir together. With so many people away on war service, it was difficult to get a balanced choir, but this was achieved. Apart from the music side, Mr Robertson also introduced Drama into the Sunday school and produced several plays – 'Ruth', 'Pilgrim's Progress' and other shorter biblical one – act plays, either in Church or Church Hall. Some pictures of these are still to be found.

Mr Robertson, through his expertise in producing such events with children, sought to instil in them the art of voice production, the art of acting out a part, and above all the very nature of the pieces in which they were involved.

Such events made a lasting impact on most of the children. Mr Gordon Ingram says ... 'He was a man before his time'. With hindsight, many more pupils would echo this sentiment. He was not only a top class Classics Master, but he had a vision for the future. One can recollect his excellent English classes, the lovely poetry which was read together and which he expounded – Latin poetry also – his love of history. He also had a great love of Greek and this he taught to a few of the senior pupils.

Mr Robertson was also a lover of Robert Burns and in class would speak the verses from 'The Cottar's Saturday Night' or any of the other poems which were being studied. On Empire Day – 24th May – there was a service in the large hall, the main part of which was the Pageant of Poetry. This covered several poems of great national feeling and those who were chosen to recite had sometimes only two days or a weekend to memorise all the words. The Headmaster spent time, in his private room, going over each line and word with the speaker so that the words and meaning came clearly across to the listeners.

There were people invited to address the school on suitable subjects. Everyone saluted the Union Jack, which was hung in the hall, and sang time honoured, stirring hymns. Mr Robertson had a great love of King and Country and was not afraid to instil in pupils that, although we were Scottish, we were part of Great Britain. The Union Jack flew from the mast on top of the school and the pupils had an afternoon holiday.

Many teachers remained permanent through the thirties and forties – Miss Jeannie Bremner, Miss Argo, Miss Fraser, Miss Elsie Harper and Miss Christina Gordon in the Primary. Earlier, the names of Miss Yeats and Miss Hardie made a strong impression upon the pupils. All of these ladies were very good teachers, some with a stronger desire than others to produce the strap and be really hard disciplinarians – sometimes a bit too hard on those who did not have the ability to absorb and learn so quickly.

In the Higher Grade or Secondary school, names such as John R. Gall immediately spring to mind. He was the pillar of the Mathematics and Science classes – a man with great tolerance, quiet dignity and an excellent way of teaching. For many he unravelled the mystery of algebra, geometry, trigonometry and the more advanced stages of Mathematics, besides the more intricate world of Science. He was very good on the discipline side as well and sometimes, when some of the older boys required to be chastised, they were passed on to Mr Gall for the punishment to be meted out. He did not often lose his temper, but when he did, it was short, quietly expressed and that was the end of the matter.

Another senior teacher was Miss Annie Melvin (later to be Mrs Cruickshank), who taught French and German. Miss Henderson was also an excellent teacher of English. She assisted Mr Robertson in the rehearsals for the Shakespeare plays, and took pupils through their words many nights after school. Miss Henderson left in the early 1940's to go to the Central school in Aberdeen. Many pupils were grateful to be taught English by the Headmaster, as they entered the Higher classes to sit the Higher Leaving Certificate. Latin was taught by Mr Norman Clark who, with Mr Donald J. Baillie, the early Mathematics teacher, was called up for war service. During the interim, a Mr Duncan, who only had one arm, taught Latin. The Headmaster also taught Latin to the senior pupils. The Art teacher for many years was Miss Margaret Mitchell. There were other, short-term teachers, from time to time. One of the very well liked Cookery teachers was Miss Selbie from Inverurie.

Miss Jessie Reid came from Monymusk to take Physical Instruction and she also became one of the Officers for the Girls' Training Corps, which started up during the war, meeting twice weekly in the school. At the same time, the Army Cadet Force came into being, and the Air Training Corps. All the young people from about fifteen years of age joined these organisations, which really were set up to prepare them for call-up. As the war went on, it became a normal thing for senior boys,when they reached the age of 18, to receive their calling-up papers and they went off to fight without ever having been employed in a job. Those who were able to, when the war was over, came back to take up their careers either at College or University, or in whatever trade or work they wanted to do. At times it was a very sad era, with the lists of names in the paper each day – killed, missing, prisoners-of-war, wounded, etc. This did bring home to the pupils that the country was at war. At school, gas mask drill was carried out each day and pupils practised getting under desks as quickly as possible. The school had an appalling smell for some time when the authorities had all the window panes covered with a thick net, which was glued on with the most evil-smelling liquid. Large black-outs were also part of the scene – these were mostly on frames which fitted into the windows. School life went on as usual and Mr Robertson, as already stated, passed on to the pupils the love of country and true patriotism.

In the early years, 1939–40, another pupil (Mary H. Duncan) recalls that in Miss Gordon's class in particular, all the boys and girls who could knit produced thick knit socks, balaclavas, etc. for the men at the front. The Red Cross supplied the wool and everyone put a little slip with their name and address on their piece of knitting. Many pupils had postcards or letters of thanks from the men who received the socks etc., many being soldiers in France. Another pupil (Charles Low) recalls very vividly the visit of Rear Admiral Burnett, brother of the local Laird at Kemnay House, Mr Arthur Burnett. He had been involved in protecting the Arctic convoys going to Russia from America, carrying supplies. He described how a particular convoy had been attacked by the Germans and drew precise diagrams to show the pupils how the battle was fought, with the Scharnhorst being one of the German battleships blown to pieces. It was a memorable day for all the pupils. The Rear Admiral was an unpretentious man and made a great impact on the pupils, despite his high rank and his involvement in the war.

From time to time, it is recalled that other high ranking Air Force or Army Officers would come to speak to the pupils, no doubt again with the thought that some of them would be joining the forces. Mr Arthur Burnett was himself involved, being Major in charge of the Home Guard in this area. He went to the headquarters at Inverurie almost every evening. There was a Home Guard Unit in Kemnay. A photograph of the Unit taken in 1943 appears on page 72. Many of the young boys who had left school at 15 joined the Home Guard until their call-up papers arrived when they reached the age of 18 years.

During this period an important character was Edward Ross, the school Janitor for many years. He put up with the pranks of many pupils over the years, but never really lost his temper. He quietly went about the work of stoking the boiler, cleaning out the outside toilets, keeping the playground free of icy slides in winter, shovelling snow, polishing brasses inside and generally keeping the school tidy.

The classrooms then had the old-fashioned wooden desks, set in tiers in the classrooms, which enabled all pupils to see the blackboard and the teacher. The infants started off with slate pencils (skillies they were called) often squeaking as the children wrote with them on their slates. Later, they moved on to write with pencils (these were triangular for easy holding), and the ability to write in joined-up letters grew. Pen and ink was the next step, the old-fashioned pens with nibs of different size on each desk.

Kemnay Platoon Home Guard 1939 – 1945

The picture of the Home Guard Platoon was taken standing on the lawn at the back of Kemnay House one Sunday morning, in the summer of 1943 after an all night exercise.

Back Row (left to Right):
James C. Law, Allan Bell, Mr Sanster 2nd horseman Nether Coullie: George Urquhart, Douglas Dow, D Rennie (Milton), James Rainnie, Dod Ewen, A Benzie, George Taylor (Paddy), John Duncan, Robert Dow, David Kemp Woodlands: W Brown (Condy).
4th Row:
W Main, A Thow, C. Thomson Overton, James Rettie, W. G. Downie, Forbes Donald, Sandy Cook, W Fraser (Walk), George Morrison, W Berry (Gooser), E. A. McPherson (Tom), Frank Adam, James Reid (Sparra) Stoneyfield.
3rd Row:
Alex Morrison, horseman at Milton, Jim Reid, Dod Malcolm, Alex M. Gordon, Joe Thomson, George Mearns, Jack Fraser, Bill Murray, William Sharp, Henry Smith, Charles Wilson, Peter Ross, Dod Clyne, Ben Ewen.
2nd Row (Seated):
E Christie (Ned) butcher, James Gibb (Curly), Archie Nicol, RSM Burns (Regular), J. R. Gall, A. M. Burnett (Laird), James Wood, James Allan, Peter Nicol, Peter Dunbar, Coder Ross, Forbes W. Findlater, George Duncan.
Front Row:
A. Brown Star House Co-op butcher, Derek Sang, Henry Cranna, Bob Donald, Jim Fraser, Walter Daun, George Gordon, Alex Dunbar, George Clark and Harry Sharp.

One pupil, in the early days of Mr Robertson – Janet McNicol (now Mrs Janet Buchan) came all the way from Glenbucket to attend Kemnay Secondary school. This meant she had to have lodgings in the village. She did very well at school, being school Dux in 1928. She then went on to Teacher Training College in Aberdeen, having a Bursary of £20 p.a. which increased to £25 in her second year. Having to pay for accommodation in the College, she was left with practically no money, not even a spare penny for a bus fare. This situation would have been reflected in the lives of many students of that era, but nevertheless, through sheer determination, those students made the grade either at College or University and many of them went into the teaching profession.

Over the years, Kemnay Secondary school produced many pupils who became professional people in all walks of life, and those who did not seek further learning made their mark too – as masons, joiners, blacksmiths, engineers, electricians. Very many of the girls who were taught at Kemnay entered the nursing profession, coping with the hard work as it was in the earlier years and rising to posts of Sister or Matron. If a record were to be drawn up, Kemnay would rate very highly in pupil achievement, not only in Mr Robertson's time, but in the earlier years of the school.

Numbers in the senior classes were dropping however, due to some pupils going on to other schools, such as fee-paying schools in Aberdeen (e.g.Robert Gordon's College). On Dr. Robertson's retirement, the school became a Junior Secondary and in later years only a Primary. Inverurie Academy then claimed the Higher Grade pupils. Kemnay Academy exists again, on a different site within the village, drawing pupils once more from a large area.

A newspaper report, on Dr. Robertson's retiral, read:

> It was touchingly appropriate that this great pioneer of school Shakespeare performances, should choose as his parting gift to a grateful public, the play that was Shakespeare's own farewell – 'The Tempest'. 'Our revels now are ended' said Prospero. Dr. Robertson has been Kemnay's Prospero, a powerful magician, under whose spell all the misgivings of those who supposed that the Swan of Avon could not spread his wings in the stolid North have been swept away.
> In the last twenty five years the proceeds of the annual open-air Shakespeare performances bought all the school prizes, equipped a school library, paid for the organised games and furnished a substantial part of the school building.

All through his years, school prizes were given in each class at the end of the summer term. For example, there was the Miss Yeats Dux Prize, the Dr. Davidson Dux Prize – the first for the Primary and the second for the Senior (Sixth Year) Dux Prize. A tribute from a former teacher at Kemnay, Father John Shand, says that J. Minto Robertson was a fine scholar with a love of literature and drama. When Father Shand moved to Edinburgh, Fettes College was in his parish there and the contrast with Kemnay Secondary school forced him to think more deeply about just what it is we are doing when trying to educate young people – it forced him to try and evaluate the strengths and weaknesses of different schools. Later in South Africa, as Head of St. John's College, then Director of Religious Education in the Diocese of Johannesburg, the warmth and friendliness, the human relationships between teachers and pupils at Kemnay, deeply influenced all he tried to do. So Kemnay school spread its spirit, not just to Donside, but to an entirely different part of the world.

Father Shand remembers especially Kemnay school daily assembly, which followed a fixed pattern – always conducted by the Head himself and always quietly, deeply reverent. This then echoes the appellation by Dr. Robertson's daughter, Margaret – "he was a truly Christian Headmaster"

John Minto Robertson – Appreciations from the Aberdeen University Review

To write adequately of John Minto Robertson is not easy. To do for him as he did so well for so many who had fallen by the way is a task impossible for one not endowed with his unusual qualities of head and heart. The attempt here made, pietatis causa, is but an old friend's tribute, partial perhaps and certainly incomplete, to the memory of a remarkable man.

The story of his life may be briefly told. He was born at Aberdeen on 3 June 1883, the son of John G. Robertson, coal manager, 184 Mid Stocket Road. He was educated at Aberdeen Grammar school, and gained seventeenth place in the Bursary Competition of 1901, out of 155 candidates, scoring the highest mark in Greek, 351 out of 400. As a member of the 1901–05 Arts Class he was a leading prizeman in English, Latin, and Greek, and in 1905 graduated M.A. with honours in Classics. Thereafter he was appointed teacher in Forfar Academy, December 1905; classical master in Albyn Place school, Aberdeen, September 1906; classical master in Turriff Higher Grade school, December 1908; and headmaster of Kemnay Secondary school in 1923. Here he continued until his retirement in 1948. Little perhaps in all this to make it clear to one who did not know him why his Alma Mater in 1945 conferred on him the honorary degree of LL.D., or why in February 1949 he was appointed editor of the Aberdeen University Review, of which he was one of the original founders.

On 11th January 1951 he died suddenly at his home, 9 Woodend Place, Aberdeen. He is survived by his wife (formerly Miss Edith J. Morrison) and by a son and two daughters, one of whom is wife of the Rector of St. Congans, Turriff.

There was not much in our beginnings to suggest that a friendship would spring up between us which was to last for well-nigh half a century. Things indeed rather pointed in the other direction. He, for instance, was town-bred; I was, as he might have put it, Turrigena, native of a place he may have known merely by name for George Ritchie of Turriff was on the staff of his school. He, of course, was "Grammar"; I, for my last year at school, was "Gordon's", and there was keen rivalry between the two institutions. By nature's contrivance, I was born a little Liberal, he a little Conservative; and in our student days we were great politicians. Finally, he was "Auld Kirk" and I was "Free", a real enough distinction fifty years ago. At the University these differences were by no means obliterated – and indeed, why should they have been? – but they were merged in the greater unity of the Class, for in our Year the class spirit was unusually strong. The fixed curriculum had by then disappeared, but in the Bursary Competition nearly all of us had taken English, Mathematics, Latin, and Greek as four of our five subjects, and to that extent had a common background. This bond was further strengthened by the fact that we were fellow members of the Honours Classics group, a small, devoted band which finally dwindled to four, the other two who stayed the course being the brilliant Netta Gordon of Kemnay, the first lady bursar at the incredible age of fifteen, and George J. Milne, oldest and steadiest of us all, who after graduating went from strength to strength and crowned a distinguished scholastic career as head of the largest secondary school in Banffshire. Within this little group, there was, as J. M. R. often recalled, great rivalry, great understanding, and great friendship.

In our first session what most impressed me in Minto Robertson was not his success in the Latin and Greek classes (that I was prepared for) but his achievement in English. I myself, efficiently crammed by a master of the art, had scored the top mark, 344 out of 400, in that subject, and in the English class I just managed to "swot" my way into the prize-list. But the penalty I paid was that I had only a meagre first-hand acquaintance with English literature and little or no understanding of what was meant by style. Not so with Minto Robertson. One day our professor, no less a person than Sir Herbert Grierson, still happily with us, set us as an optional exercise an essay in the style of Addison. I gave up the attempt in despair; to Robertson, as they say round Glasgow way, it was "nae bother". At the end of the session he was first prizeman in a strong class, and facile princeps at that. Here I state my firm conviction that, fine classic as he was, if he had chosen rather to study for honours in English he had it in him to become one of the best English scholars of his generation. Our small honours group was not a little overshadowed by our immediate predecessors, particularly by that mighty triumvirate, two years our senior, W. M. Calder, Alexander Petrie, and John Fraser, who in that order won three consecutive Ferguson Scholarships in Classics, a feat which may never be equalled. These and others of our older contemporaries won open scholarships or exhibitions which carried them to Oxford or Cambridge, and we too sought to follow them, non passibus aequis. Minto Robertson, with a courage which I admired, sought thus in his final year to enter Balliol, then regarded as the most difficult of all the Oxford colleges to get into – Balliol did not receive him, and so threw away the chance of producing another MacKail or – who knows ? – another Grierson.

In our student days we who lived in "digs" seldom met our town colleagues in their homes. Of the four which I had the privilege of entering one was the home of the Robertsons. I remember his father as a dark-bearded, rather spare man, with a surprisingly resonant voice, which left me in no doubt whence came Minto's own deep, melodious baritone. Facially he resembled his mother, whose smiling welcome still clings to my memory. Where we undergraduates did most often foregather was at Marischal College on Friday evenings, when most of the Societies had their meetings. Minto was a prominent member of the Debating, Choral, and Literary Societies, and it was in the last of these that he was most interested. In his second year he held the secretaryship, an office in which I succeeded him, and in our last year he was president. In a note on Dr. Herbert Wiseman (A.U.R., Autumn 1950, p488) he refers to Gavin Greig's lecture on Prince Charlie, and mentions that it was "the writer" (anonymous, but unmistakable!) who was responsible for this innovation of music to widen the appeal of literature and history. I should like to tell a little of what lay behind this "innovation" because it will illustrate certain traits in his character which I for one found stimulating and engaging. To be closely associated with him in those days was not a dull experience. For there was in him a gay insouciance, a readiness at times to leap and not look, where cannier comrades might look and not leap at all, something original, impulsive, unpredictable. The "Literary" then, had for some time been in failing health; in our third year, as Alex. Petrie, humorist as well as classic, once said in another connection, it had fallen into a coma and was in danger of coming to a full stop. Minto, who had the interests of the Society much at heart, decided that a blood transfusion was necessary. One Friday night, after the lecturer sat down, he rose to open the usual discussion, and before the audience quite realized it, he had worked round to the subject of his new proposals. Of course, he was entirely out of order; there was a stormy scene, and the meeting stood adjourned, but not before he had threatened to leave the Society and found a new one of his own. False, I suppose to my Free Kirk upbringing, I strove to prevent a disruption of the Society, and he was too good a man for it to lose. The disentangling of the knot called, it seemed, for quiet, calm, deliberation and so, a few days later, we two argued out the matter as we walked together all the way from King's to Mid Stocket Road, and reached agreement – a perfect example of solvitur ambulando. It was all so typical of the man – resolute to achieve his end but ready to compromise on the means. At the adjourned meeting he was elected president for the ensuing session; two of our most distinguished students, George Herbert Mair and Herbert Wiseman, were appointed, secretary and sub-secretary respectively; and with three men of that calibre in control is it surprising that 1904-05 was something of an annus mirabilis in the history of the Society?

I have dealt at some length with Minto Robertson's student days for two reasons, first, because a notable man's beginnings are always interesting, perhaps the most interesting thing about him, and, secondly, because he was one who matured early, as geniuses and near-geniuses are wont to do. As he was then, so he remained through life, developing and mellowing but essentially the same. During his fifteen years of the classical mastership at Turriff we did not often meet. My work was in Aberdeen, and the 1914-18 war separated us still further. But from family and common friends came constant information of his doings both in and out of school.

For reasons, both personal and other, then, I was more than delighted when Minto Robertson, then in the prime of life, was by the wise decision of Aberdeenshire Education Authority given charge of Kemnay Secondary school. Something unusual, I felt, was sure to happen there, and happen it did. I am not competent to speak of those Shakespeare productions whose fame was soon to spread far and wide beyond the confines of Kemnay and the North-East. I was never able to witness any of these performances, but I heard enough about them to realize how much I was missing. It was a unique experiment in education at its very best, original in conception and of great and lasting value to all, performers and audience alike, who were privileged to be there. I can, I think, with reasonable certainty conjecture something of what was in Minto Robertson's mind when he embarked on this great experiment. Had he merely wanted his pupils to become acquainted with Shakespeare, he could have had them crammed for the purpose, though I cannot imagine him doing or allowing anything of the sort. Had he wished them to understand and appreciate Shakespeare, good class-teaching would have sufficed. But even that would not satisfy so enthusiastic a Shakespearean. He would re-create Shakespeare for his pupils, bring him to new life for them, make them enjoy him in speech and action, and communicate that joy to their audience. And, as though that were not enough, he would do all this, not in a conventional setting, but, whenever possible, in the open air. Without any doubt, his true intent was all for their delight. It seems only his due that I should here give wider currency to what I said of him when proposing the toast of the Class at our eighth reunion on 21 October 1949: "If there is any member of our year of whom it may be truly said that he had a touch of genius, it is surely the man who for a quarter of a century produced that wonderful series of Shakespeare plays, and whom his Alma Mater so worthily honoured by conferring on him the highest distinction which she has it in her power to bestow". These words were acclaimed by all of his twenty classmates there assembled, and those who read them now will not deem them undeserved.

Happy as Minto Robertson was in Turriff and in Kemnay, and sorry as he was to part from these communities, happier still, I am sure, he was to return to his native Bon-Accord, and beyond any doubt happiest of all in his brief and brilliant editorship of the Review. For here was work after his own heart, work which gave him ample scope, work for which he was specially qualified; and for which he will be remembered with gratitude and affection.

It was a hard task he had undertaken. The compilation and presentation of items under such headings as University News, Olim Cives, Hymeneal, and Personalia must have been a laborious labour of love; he cast his net wide to secure original contributions on many subjects, literary, musical, scientific, antiquarian; there were reviews and memoirs to arrange for; and, finally, to leaven it all and make the Review the yeasty, living thing it was, came the genial, witty, humorous, yet serious editor himself, surveying the human scene through his World Window, reviewing critically and sympathetically men and books, and at times, doctoral gown discarded for student toga, indulging in a sparkling jeu d'esprit and punning his way shamelessly in Greek, English, and "Buchan" from the heroes and heroines of classical mythology down to Wimbledon and what he called the new pantisocracy. And, as I have already indicated, it mattered little whether he wrote anonymously or otherwise; the Robertsonian touch was always there, unique and unmistakable, for it mirrored the man himself. Although, as I have said, he matured early, he was not acting out of character in thus assuming on occasion the toga iuvenilis. He never outgrew or suppressed the boyish element that was in him; shades of the prison-house never did entirely close upon him. And yet, with all that buoyancy of spirit which kept him from sinking in our modern sea of troubles, he could look with serious eyes through his World Window. No melancholy Jaques, he did not ask to be invested with his motley – motley was not his wear – but he did ask, and take, leave to speak his mind and even to prescribe his remedy for the infected world. Even such as would not patiently receive his medicine could not fail to be charmed by the kindly and learned doctor's bedside manner.

Bright is the ring of words when the right man rings them. Minto Robertson was a born writer, the right man indeed when he had something to say. He ranged easily and confidently over classical and modern literature, and from his prodigious memory he could always produce the apt, felicitous quotation. Notwithstanding his own disclaimer, there was in him a little of the poet. This is how he began his moving tribute to another great character, our well-loved class-fellow, John Keith Forbes, "Student and Sniper-Sergeant", who fell in Flanders on 25 September 1915:

> Last week was a week of rainbows, with, on Friday, a perfect one, spanning the whole heavens in one magnificent arch, seeming a fit bridge for passing to Valhalla of the great-hearted heroes who had just died on the battle-field of France, seeming, too, a fit poising-place for the Valkyries to chant their own hymn, "Glory to Thor in the highest – on earth War".

And he ended thus:

> Now all that throbbing life-force is still. Another bright flame is quenched. The many musical instruments are silent, the tent, companion of his tours, is folded; the Hebrew oracles are dumb. But elsewhere, we may believe, "in the labour-house vast of Being", his activity has not ceased. We may think of him now practising with harp and psaltery; we may imagine him now pitching his tabernacle in other Highlands, and, his initiation in the Hebrew oracles completed, essaying now the very Mount of God.

Were these, as he himself said, the level tones of prose? I doubt it. Minto and I forgathered for the last time by his own fire-side. It was on an autumn evening of last year, and we talked far into the small hours. Like Aeneas and Achates, the two old friends

multa inter sese vario sermone serebant.

Much of our varied interchange of talk was of the past, but he would not dwell too long on that. Rather would he speak of things present and to come, of the next Review and of the next gathering of the Class. It was he who had called us to our reunion in 1949; already he was planning a golden jubilee assembly in 1951. But dis aliter visum.

And now, with infinite affection and regret, we of his Class who still face the light join with the greater family of Alumni, whom he was surely drawing together in a stronger devotion to our common Alma Mater, and with all his other friends everywhere, in bidding him a sad, reluctant farewell.

Invitis nobis frater adempte, vale.

A. J. Smith (M.A. 1905, D.Litt. 1919).

Dr. Robertson, scholar, gentleman, teacher, lover of drama, was a product of two centuries. There was a flavour of Victorianism in his courtesy and charm of manner, while at the same time his sympathies lay with the most modern of educationists, even to the abolishing of hated examinations.

"This is Arden", said Dr. Robertson on viewing for the first time the glorious woods which surrounded his school at Kemnay, and he was not content until he made his Arden ring with the voices of Portia, Cleopatra, Shylock, Lear, and so many more of his beloved Shakespeare characters. Many of us will remember the 400 years old beech tree in the grounds of Kemnay House where, year after year, the plays were unfolded, now with dignity, now with rollicking wholesome fun. It was the man behind the productions who gave them their unqualified success, for Dr. Robertson had the gift of rendering dignified and convincing the serious roles, and of frolicking unrestrainedly with the clowns.

"Disce Vivere" was the motto chosen by Dr. Robertson for his pupils, and his noble aim as a teacher was to initiate the young people under his care into a fuller way of life. His first aim was to establish a library and to make the children love books as he himself did. "Tolle lege; tolle lege" ran the inviting superscription on one of his book-cases. On another: "Vita Hominum Sine Literis Mors Est". Thus wide fields of literature were opened for exploration.

In the classroom, too, the dramatic element was felt. The Classics became alive. Under Dr. Robertson's expert teaching Cicero really lived and declaimed as from a modern platform. Caesar was the conquering hero. "Ecce Caesar, ecce Caesar, qui subegit Gallias" chanted the pupils. Greek, which Dr. Robertson so loved, was taught but to the chosen few, but all became familiar with the myths of Greece and Rome. While revering the Classics, Dr. Robertson admired the clarity of modern French, he was familiar with Italian and tolerated German, which he goodnaturedly termed barbarian. "Stille Nacht" was a favourite carol every Christmas, whether in its original form or as "Sainte Nuit" or "Still the Night". Another subject which Dr. Robertson successfully taught and of which he made a special study was History. Poetry with him became a thing of beauty, surely because he so loved the poets himself and kept forever his eyes of wonder.

Allied with all this was Dr. Robertson's love of music, Chopin being his favourite composer. He was no mean musician himself and when desired, could take his place at the church organ and fill the air with the strains of his beloved "Largo". Dr. Robertson was also notable as a public speaker and had indeed a command of the English language, whether spontaneous or studied, which was almost unparalleled. His was the true culture which links all the arts.

Nor must we forget the deep religious feeling which permeated his life. The daily morning service was an act of devotion. The children came to learn and love a wide choice of beautiful hymns and the finest of the psalms, and the headmaster's powerful bass was a fitting accompaniment to the treble of the young voices. There was also a daily reading from the Bible and so the Book became better known in Dr. Robertson's school than it is reputed to be in many parts of our country at the present day. Dr. Robertson was an elder of the Church and leader of the Sunday school. It is not surprising therefore that he was tempted to produce sacred as well as secular plays. First came The Pilgrim's Progress, then Ruth, The Finding of the King, and several others.

It was fitting that his Alma Mater should confer on this eminent scholar her highest honour of Doctor of Laws. A few years after receiving this degree Dr. Robertson retired from active teaching, but he did not retire from his literary activities, although failing health, alas, made his motto "Festina lente". Under the pen-name of Epimetheus he kept on contributing articles, full of his own refreshing humour, to the Educational Journal. He completed the Statistical Account of Kemnay; he was working on the Roll of Honour of the University and had undertaken the editing of the University Review when his life was suddenly cut off.

We mourn the passing of a cultured scholar, a fine gentleman, and an enterprising and tolerant headmaster, but we are left with a wealth of fragrant memories. We are tempted to make a slight adaptation of Hamlet's lines and apply them to Dr. Robertson: "He was a man, take him for all in all, we shall not look upon his like again".

A. Cruickshank (Annie Melvin, M.A. 1929).

Mr and Mrs J Minto Robertson at the Schoolhouse door

Kemnay Secondary School

Taken on the occasion of King George V's Silver Jubilee in 1935. A national holiday was declared for the event and the photograph includes the school pupils along with the Scouts and Guides. Mr J. Minto Robertson is on the left in the light suit. An enlargement of this photograph hung for many years in the small hall.

Class Photograph of 1911

Miss Adam standings to the left is the teacher of this rather large class.

Class Photograph of 1922

Back Row (left to right): *Name Unknown, Name Unknown*, John Philip, Bob Dow, Colin Begg, Leslie Adams, Billy Walker, *Name Unknown*. 3rd Row: Joy Inglis, Sammy Lawrence, John Gardiner, John Wood, John Stuart, John Gilmore, Melva Smith. 2nd Row: *Name Unknown, Name Unknown*, Margo Reid, Alice Innes, Margaret Mitchell, Margaret Adams, *Name Unknown*, Elsie Connon, May Knowles. Front Row: Annie Milne, *Name Unknown*, Mac Barnett, Margaret Petrie, Annie Elrick and Miss Fraser (Dainty Dinah).

Kemnay Secondary School, Junior Infants intake April 1933.

Back Row: Wm Connon, John Clarihew, *Name Unknown*, Alexander (Sandy) Gall, Harry Brown, *Name Unknown*, Wm Ross, *Name Unknown*. Middle Row: Wm Clark, Alex Cheyne, Robert Ross, John McNaughton, James Smith. Front Row: Mary H. Duncan, Annie D. Ferries, Sheila Wight, Sheila Adams, Annie (Nan) McCombie, Evelyn Cranna and Eliz. (Elma) M. Cook.

Kemnay School Percussion Band 1945

Back Row: Billy Weir, Margaret Downie, Ian Wallace, Alice McPherson, Evelyn Lyon, George Daun. Front Row: Jean Gordon Conductor, Duncan Lyon, Alfie Anderson, Melvyn Clyne, Isobel Pirie, Joyce Lyon, Sonia Gordon, James Downie, Douglas Pickford, Margart Grant and Sheena Grant.

A Typical School Report Card for 1933

Teachers

Historically, the movement of members of staff from one school to another was very limited. Living away from home, in lodgings or rented accommodation, placed a heavy strain on finance bearing in mind the level of salaries. Public transport, apart from the railway, was practically non-existent. Kemnay School had its share of long-serving members of staff, particularly in the primary department, some of whom gave a lifetime of service to the school. Many are still remembered by former pupils, although a century has elapsed since their names first appeared in the school records.

As long ago as 1894, Miss Christina Hardie and Miss Jane Bremner applied for a vacancy as a pupil teacher. Miss Bremner was considered too young at the time, and Miss Hardie was duly appointed. Miss Bremner was subsequently appointed to a similar post, and both continued to serve as pupil teachers until the time came for them to enter college. Miss Hardie returned to Kemnay at a salary of £37, where she was to become an efficient member of staff, until her untimely death in 1930. She will be remembered as a strict disciplinarian, who served for a number of years in the dual role as teacher in the primary school, whilst also instructing in "drawing" (later to be termed "art"), pupils in the secondary department who were at Leaving Certificate stage.

After serving as a pupil teacher, Jeannie Bremner left Kemnay School and entered college in Aberdeen in 1899. On leaving college, Miss Bremner spent a brief spell at Barthol Chapel, but returned to Kemnay in July 1904, to teach in the senior section. She was the daughter of William Bremner of Alehousewells, a man who took a great interest in the school. Being a surveyor to trade, he had acted as overseer to the school board at some of the school extensions. He was also responsible for the planning of the buildings occupied by the Clydesdale Bank in the High Street.

Miss Bremner was appointed infant mistress in 1910, where she remained for the rest of her teaching life, to guide through their initial year at school, hundreds of Kemnay children stretching to two or even three generations. For a period, too, Miss Bremner took charge of music in the "Higher Grade". She was due to retire in 1945, but owing to the shortage of teachers, the Director asked her to continue. In the inspector's report for session 1945–46, we read:

'Infant and Primary Divisions. In the lower infant room, where the teacher combines long experience with an enlightened and progressive outlook, a firm foundation has been laid in reading and in number, and swift writing was of good quality.'

She continued teaching until 1951 when she retired following a spell of ill health. On that occasion, she was entertained to dinner in the Northern Hotel, Aberdeen, by her colleagues on 26th June, where she was presented with a brown morocco handbag. On the evening of June 29th, a public presentation was made at the school where she received a mahogany bureau and a gold bracelet from friends and former pupils. The address was given by Mr James Downie, Kirkstyle, and Mrs Weir, Blythewood made the presentation. The headmaster presided over the meeting. Tea was served and a short musical programme was provided by the pupils under Mrs Cowe, teacher of singing, and Miss Harper. Following her death in August 1958, at the age of seventy nine years, she left a legacy of £200 to the school as a prize fund.

Miss Sophie Yeats was appointed an assistant teacher in 1895, straight from the Free Church Training College in Aberdeen. A few years later, she took charge of the pupils in Standard V, at that time the senior class in the primary department. She was to continue in this post until she retired in 1932, having been responsible for the preparation of many pupils for the secondary department. Gentle but firm, Miss Yeats was held in high esteem by staff and pupils alike, having spent her entire teaching life at Kemnay. She endowed two prizes at the school, the Miss Yeats Prize being awarded to the dux of the primary school, and the other awarded to the pupil making most progress in Class V. She retired to Edinburgh, where she died on 11th March 1937.

Miss Christina Smith Gordon, more commonly known as Kirsty, joined the staff as teacher of Senior II on 3rd December 1917. She took on the teaching of the qualifying class on the retiral of Miss Yeats, where she remained for the rest of her teaching career. She retired on 1st July 1955 after thirty eight years on the staff and twenty three years as teacher of the highest class in the primary department. She was also in charge of the School Savings for twenty two years. She was an excellent teacher, but of a somewhat eccentric nature. During the week she lodged in the village, travelling home to Clatt at the weekend. On one occasion, a severe snowstorm blew up over the weekend, closing all routes in the area. Her class was looking forward to a

Kemnay School Staff May 2nd 1947

Back Row (left to right): Mr Donald Baillie (assistant in Maths and Science and Geography Master), Mr Norman Clark (Classical Master), Miss Jessie Reid (Physical Education), Miss Meta Forbes (Domestic Science), Miss Isobel Douglas (English), Mr John R. Gall (Principal teacher of Maths and Science) and Mr Edward Ross (Janitor). Front Row: Miss Margaret Melvin (Assistant Infant Mistress and Primary I), Miss Jessie Fraser (Primary II and III), Miss Christina S. Gordon (Primary V Qualifying class), Dr J. Minto Robertson (Headmaster), Miss Jeannie Brenner (Infant Mistress), Miss Elsie Harper (Primary III and IV), Miss Jessie Minty (Principal teacher of Modern Languages).

day's break, but Miss Gordon appeared on Monday, having walked all the way from Clatt, some 20 miles.

Another long serving teacher in the primary was Miss Jessie D. Fraser who started work on November 11th 1918. She taught in the primary department until 1947 when she was transferred to Alford. Commonly known as "Dainty Dinah", she was well liked by all those who passed through her class. Another of that era was Miss Argo who stayed at Kintore and travelled to school by motor cycle.

Miss Elsie Harper joined the staff in May 1932 to teach Primary IV when Miss Gordon took over the Qualifying class. She had previously taught at Monymusk since 1913. When door to door collections were held in the community, these were usually taken by school pupils organised by Miss Harper. She was often involved in musical work with the children. A quiet, popular teacher, she retired in June 1959.

Almost an institution in the senior school was John Reid Gall M.A. (Hons) who took up the post of teacher of Mathematics and Science on 9th June 1919. He retired as principal teacher of these subjects on June 29th 1956 after thirty seven years on the staff. A strict disciplinarian, he was held in high esteem by those whom he taught.

The School Activities Fund

The income from this worthwhile fund was derived from various sources, the main fund raising event being the annual Shakespeare play. Many items were purchased from the proceeds, which would not otherwise have been available to the pupils of those days. In the school log book of the twenties and the thirties are recorded some of the uses e.g. all the prizes which were presented at the close of the school year with the exception of a few endowed awards; for the boys 'an entire outfit for the football team one dozen jerseys, one dozen pairs of pants and a football'; and for the girls 'one dozen hockey sticks, guards and a ball' at a cost of £13 5s; for those participating in the music festival in Aberdeen, lunch at one shilling each and tea at ninepence, the pupils having paid their own bus fares. Later, 32 new framed photographs were purchased to hang in the main hall, costing £9 15s; the first school radio; a cine projector which attracted a grant of £15, and in January 1948, 'a new amplifier system, wired to the hall and to all the classrooms at a cost of £84' which, according to the log book, was reputed to be the first to be installed in an Aberdeenshire school.

Lighting and Heating

By present day standards, the lighting and heating systems were somewhat primitive. In the 1920s and 30s, the coal fired central heating system was effective but unpredictable. Breakdowns occurred regularly, and it is recorded in 1933 that 116 leaks in the system were repaired. Lighting was provided by inefficient oil lamps – one on the desk of each of the teachers. In 1930, the Director of Education called at the school to hear the Headmaster's views on his proposal that they should purchase the old lamps from Kemnay East Church, where a lighting plant had been installed. These lamps 'with circular burners and copper brackets' were purchased subsequently 'at a cost of five shillings per lamp and one shilling per bracket', and every class in school was to enjoy the luxury of lighting in winter. Electricity did not reach Kemnay until later in the decade, and indeed it was a red letter day when the new electrical installation was switched on in January 1938.

Hot Dinners

Mr Robertson was very proud of this scheme, which he inaugurated, whereby pupils, mainly from outwith the village, could enjoy a plate of soup at midday during the winter months. It is recalled that the first boiler was installed in the underground boiler house, along with the central heating furnace, with its attendant supply of coal! In 1931 a new boiler was installed in the cookery room, and this led to an increase in the numbers partaking of the "hot dinners". It is recorded that the scheme was once more 'a great success and was self-supporting at a cost of one penny per head but every pupil was not required to pay'.

A new school canteen was opened in 1948, shortly before the Headmaster retired. Meals were provided at a cost of five (old) pennies each, for the first and second members of a family, and three pence for the remainder of a family. It was typical of Dr. Robertson to take canteen duty himself on the first day, and to record in the log book that the scheme 'promises to be an unqualified success'. This despite the fact that on the first day the potato peeler refused to function, and the milk and vegetables failed to arrive!

Janitors

Janitors were of great importance in those days, and seemed to devote their entire lives to the school. In addition to their normal duties they, along with their wives, were responsible for all the cleaning work, and for preparing and serving the "hot dinners". It is recorded that in 1934, the Janitor Ed. Ross's wife was at last 'to receive direct payment from the County Council for carrying out the hot dinners scheme at a rate of three shillings per day.' (sadly Mrs Ross died at an early age some three years later).

Other duties undertaken by the janitor included the cultivation and harvesting of potatoes in the school garden, the supervision of and the collecting of the pennies from the school milk scheme, and the setting up and dismantling of the arena for the annual open air Shakespeare plays. For some of these tasks, he was assisted by the older boys, for whom it was quite an honour to be chosen to be members of Ed's squad. He would also have been expected to effect minor repairs to buildings and equipment, attend to problems with the central heating system, and trim and fill the numerous paraffin lamps. The enormity of his tasks may be gleaned from an entry in the log book at the close of the summer holidays – 'the classrooms and halls have been thoroughly cleaned and washed by the janitor, who has spent the whole vacation attending to the school'.

Storms

It was not unknown for Kemnay to be cut off from the outside world. Two severe snowstorms occurred during the war years in the early forties, and on both occasions, it is written in the log that no trains, buses, mail or newspapers reached the village for several days. On one particular day, only 76 pupils were present in the entire school. Although most of the teachers resided in the village during the week, it was quite possible for some of them to be cut off from Kemnay at weekends. On one occasion, Miss Henderson left her home in Banchory on the Sunday, spent the night in Aberdeen, eventually travelling by train to Kintore, before walking the last four miles to school in a heavy snowstorm. It is also on record that Miss Gordon, on one occasion walked much of the way from her home in Clatt, whilst Miss Fraser found it necessary to travel by lorry from Alford. Those who knew Miss Fraser will realise that she was the most unlikely person to consider such a mode of transport.

Epidemics

In common with most schools, Kemnay endured its share of epidemics over the years. One such was the outbreak of measles in December 1930. The attendance in the primary school dropped to 18%, and on one particular day, Miss Bremner found herself with only one pupil in the infant class. The Headmaster alerted the Director of Education as to the severity of the problem, which produced the curt response 'Carry on'. Another such event was the 'flu epidemic of 1937, when 132 absentees were noted on one particular day – nearly half the school roll.

Perfect Attendance

As would have been normal practice in those days, great stress was made on regular attendance, and at the prize giving ceremony in June, certificates were awarded to those pupils with perfect attendance throughout the year. In 1928, 28 such certificates were presented, including one to Alexina Forbes who had not missed a day at school for nine years, and to Kathleen Marriot for six years. Two years later, no fewer than 73 qualified for the award, including Lily Forbes with six years, and Violet Laing (who was dux of the school that year) with a remarkable ten year record. Although the issue of such certificates was discontinued some years later, the Headmaster continued to keep a record of good attendance, including the occasion on which the three members of the Connon family had a record of perfect attendance for five, seven and nine years respectively.

Individual Winners

It is obvious that in Mr Robertson's time pupils participated in competitions which were run on a national basis. Amongst those who emerged with distinction were: Violet Laing, who gained third place in her section of a UK competition in handwriting, and for which she was awarded an inscribed Waterman pen; Ella Gall, who won first place in the Royal Empire Society's essay competition open to schools throughout the Empire – the subject was 'the story of the Canadian railways' and the award, a bronze medal and books; Violet Connon, who was the winner in her section (under eleven, in an essay competition open to all schools throughout Scotland – there were 17,000 entries in her section, and at a special presentation, she was awarded eight volumes of 'The Book of Knowledge'; and a future winner in the same competition some years later was Ethel Weir who also became the recipient of the same award.

General

There were numerous other innovations during Mr Robertson's sojourn at Kemnay. A games period appeared on the timetable in 1928, and this was later increased to two periods. The participation of choirs in the annual Music Festival in Aberdeen became a regular feature, this being associated with a sightseeing tour of the city on foot, which included an ever popular visit to Woolworths. Certain proposals by the Headmaster did not materialise at the time, such as a proposition that the field adjoining the school be purchased as a playing field. This became a reality many years later. He also endeavoured to persuade the Director to include as a subject for the Day School Certificate, cookery for boys, in association with the 'Benchwork' course, again without success at the time. The school Christmas party for senior pupils and staff was instituted, at a net cost on the first occasion of four pence per pupil! A great believer in saving, he vigorously promoted the National Savings Scheme, and one of his final entries in the log records the fact that during his 25 years, the total saved amounted to £16,437. He also gave tremendous encouragement to the proposal by local musician, John Morgan, that a violin orchestra be instituted. Violins could be purchased by pupils on an instalment basis, and it is proudly recorded that there were no defaulters under the scheme. In March 1938 came the first performance of the combined schools orchestra (Kemnay, Kintore and Monymusk) with 52 violins, and the hall was reputed to be 'packed to the door'.

School Buildings

At the time of the Reformation, it was the earnest desire of the church hierarchy that a school be provided in every parish (1646 (2nd Feb.) Act for "founding of schools in everie paroche"). Eventually a bye law came into being to the effect that parochial schools had to be provided and maintained by the heritors but under the supervision of the church.

Little has been handed down to us either of these humble dwellings or their equally humble occupants. It is well known that the post of parochial schoolmaster was not very lucrative, and from what can be gleaned, his dwelling was somewhat spartan.

The parochial school of Kemnay was situated where the old schoolhouse now stands. Prior to the advent of the Turnpike road from Kintore to Alford in the early 1820's, the layout of the roads around Kemnay differed somewhat from those of today. The road from Leschangie did not swing round the side of what is now the Pleasure Park, but carried on up beside the line of beech trees leading to Greenkirtles before turning right to join up with the road that is now High Street. A track existed similar to the present route of Grove Road and Victoria Terrace. The school was situated near this cross roads.

Road layout of 1792 taken from the Kemnay Estate map. The names are the 20th century equivalents.

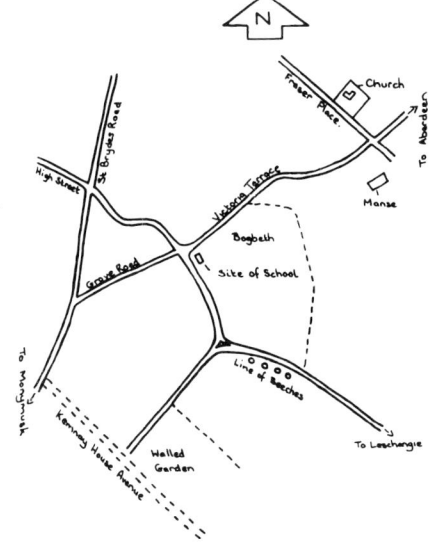

The article from *Chambers Journal* (p32) describes the school buildings at Kemnay in the early 1840's as being picturesque. That could quite possibly have been true, but on the other hand, that is the opinion of a visitor who may have viewed the situation through rose coloured spectacles. Over the period when Andrew Stevenson was at Kemnay school, he added considerably to the buildings, all at his own expense. Stevenson was not a wealthy man, nor was his salary anything but meagre. Consequently the buildings which he erected were not of a very high standard (neither, for that matter, were the other domestic buildings in the parish), but they sufficed for his needs.

In July 1855, comparative prices for thatching and slating the school and schoolhouse were submitted. In 1860, William Allan was commissioned by the laird's advocates to inspect the school property and report back. In this report the schoolroom is described as a 'wooden erection with a flat roof covered with felt and tar...' Such was the state of the roof that it was unsafe to walk on, even some of the boarding at the foundations had disappeared altogether. It also states that the dwelling house had been recently slated. The schoolhouse is described as having four rooms and a kitchen. The ceilings of the passages and two of the rooms were only six and a half feet in height and the floors were below the surrounding ground level causing dampness and other problems.

Allan recommended that although the school house accommodation may be passable, if the heritors were contemplating erecting a new schoolroom, it may be policy to demolish everything and start afresh by building a new schoolhouse as well, or at least making provision for one to be erected at a later date.

The first option was adopted and later that year, a new schoolhouse and schoolroom were erected. This consisted of the building now known as the Old Schoolhouse, along with the building at right angles to the schoolhouse. This building served the needs of the parish until the introduction of compulsory education in 1872, which decreed that all children between the ages of five and thirteen should attend school. This, coupled with the rapid increase in the local population, due to the recently opened quarries, strained the accommodation to the utmost. According to the census of 1861, the number of children between the ages of 5 and 13 attending school was 135. The corresponding figures for 1871 and 1881 were 249 and 387 respectively.

The newly elected School Board in 1873 deliberated at great length on the alternatives: to extend the existing accommodation or erect a new building.

By the meeting of 2nd January 1874, George Gellie had produced plans and specifications for proposed school buildings. These were approved by the Board and it was 'resolved to forward them as soon as convenient for the consideration of the Department'.

At the meeting held on 2nd March 1874:
'The Clerk was instructed to submit the plans of the new school buildings for the inspection of Mr Burnett the proprietor'.

'The treasurer was authorised to sign, in name of the School Board approval of the plans and specifications for the supply of water for the schools and the sanitary improvement of the village'.

The plans of the new buildings had received full sanction before the meeting of 28th April as had the Deed of Transfer. The clerk was instructed to forward all documents to their solicitor Mr Kelmo, and their architect was asked to contact the tradesmen as soon as possible to discuss modifying their estimates.

These were put to the meeting held on 6th May as follows:

Mr Fyfe as mason	£268 . .
Middleton, Carpenter	£165 . .
Rhind, Slater & Plumber	£64 .12 .9
Chisholm & Son, Plasterer	£20 .17 .9
Amounting in all to	£518 .10 .6

This building which would operate as a girls and infant school consisted of the room parallel to Grove Road at the western end of the feu, and the room adjoining it at right angles.

By 1879, accommodation was again strained and another room was added to this building consisting of about two thirds of the present hall.

This served the needs of the school until December 1886 when the Board found that the school roll was 368 whereas the buildings were only scheduled to contain 322. It was resolved to try and alleviate the situation. Again,

School Building of 1874

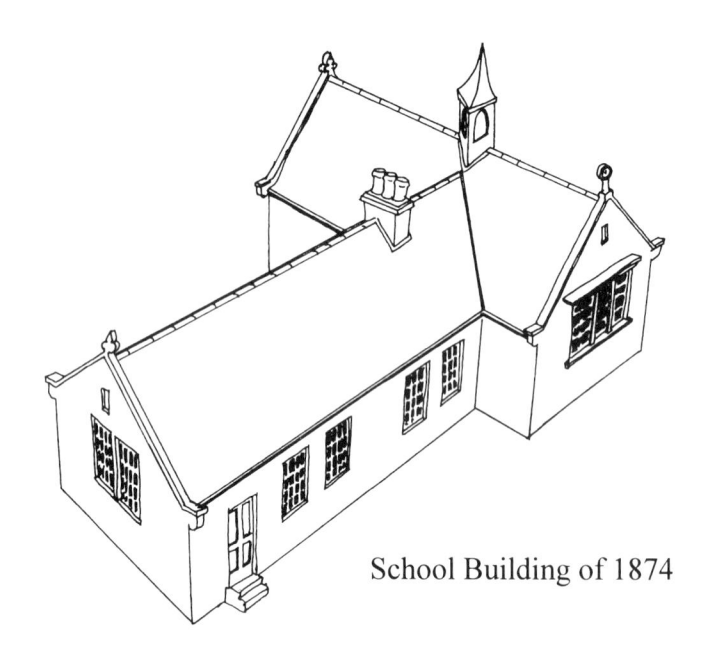

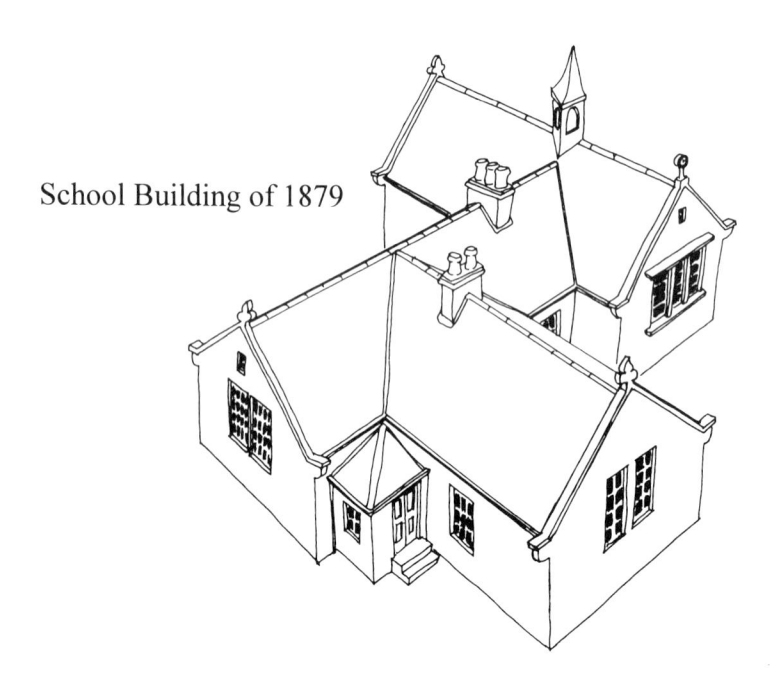

School Building of 1879

considerable discussion took place before a solution was arrived at. It was decided to add another room to the old school beside the schoolhouse. Mr Bremner of Fetternear was appointed surveyor for the works. Before the works were finished in December 1887, several alterations had been carried out to other parts of the buildings, but mostly of a minor nature.

In May 1894, it was once more resolved to extend the school. Two proposals were put forward, one of which was to extend the small room of the building to the west of the playground. The other was to extend by building across the end of the small room. The second motion was accepted, but it so happened that a tree grew at the end of the school where this building was to be erected and the laird, A. G. Burnett, refused permission to fell the tree. The situation was resolved by extending the small room some three feet and building across the end of this.

> Kemnay 29th July 1894[*]
>
> A special meeting of the Board was held today in the Public School. Present Rev. A Hood Smith, Messrs Petrie, Tawse and Taylor. Mr Taylor was appointed Chairman pro tem.
>
> The minute of the previous meeting was read and approved.
>
> The committee in connection with enlargement of the school reported that Mr Burnett the superior of the ground had refused to allow the tree at the end of the school to be cut down and that in consequence it would be impossible to construct the building as proposed. The matter having been fully considered Mr Tawse moved, 'that in order to meet the difficulty caused by the refusal of Mr Burnett of Kemnay to allow the tree at the end of the school to be taken down, an additional three feet be built to the old classroom so that the corner of the new building by being that space brought forward may clear the tree.' This was seconded by Mr Petrie and agreed to unanimously.
>
> James Taylor   Chairman pro tem.

[*] Minutes appear out of chronological order in original book.

Kemnay 17th July 1894

The tenders for the work of enlarging the school having been considered it was resolved to accept the lowest offers which are as follows. Mason Work, Mr Lubin Dinnie, Builder, Cluny on condition that he is prepared to commence operations within one week of date of acceptance and finish within four weeks from commencement. Amount of tender £120 Joiner Work, Mr Wm Wright, Builder, Bridge of Alford, amount £72.10.6 Slater, Mr Wm Auld, Kemnay, amount £329.16 Plaster Work, Mr Robert Moir, Inverurie, amount £16.19

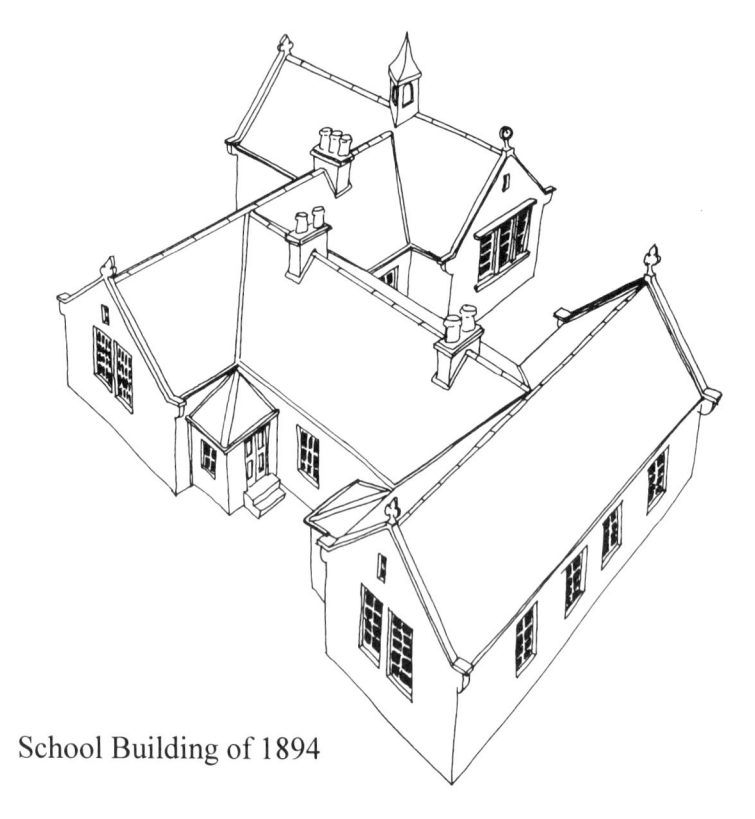

School Building of 1894

By 1899 a need was felt for additional playground area. A wall was built to enclose this extended area of ground. At the same time latrines were built and hot water circulation was installed in the school house.

The school was recognised as having a Higher Grade Department as from 1st August 1905, and Mr Kelly, Architect, Aberdeen was commissioned to draw up plans to accommodate the extra pupils this generated. The extension consisted of the large hall and the rooms opening off it. It was opened on 27th October 1906.

This extension to the school buildings served the needs of the school, albeit with the usual ongoing alterations and maintenance until after the Second World War. In 1947 the school kitchen and canteen were built as was the adjoining building which was used as the woodwork room.

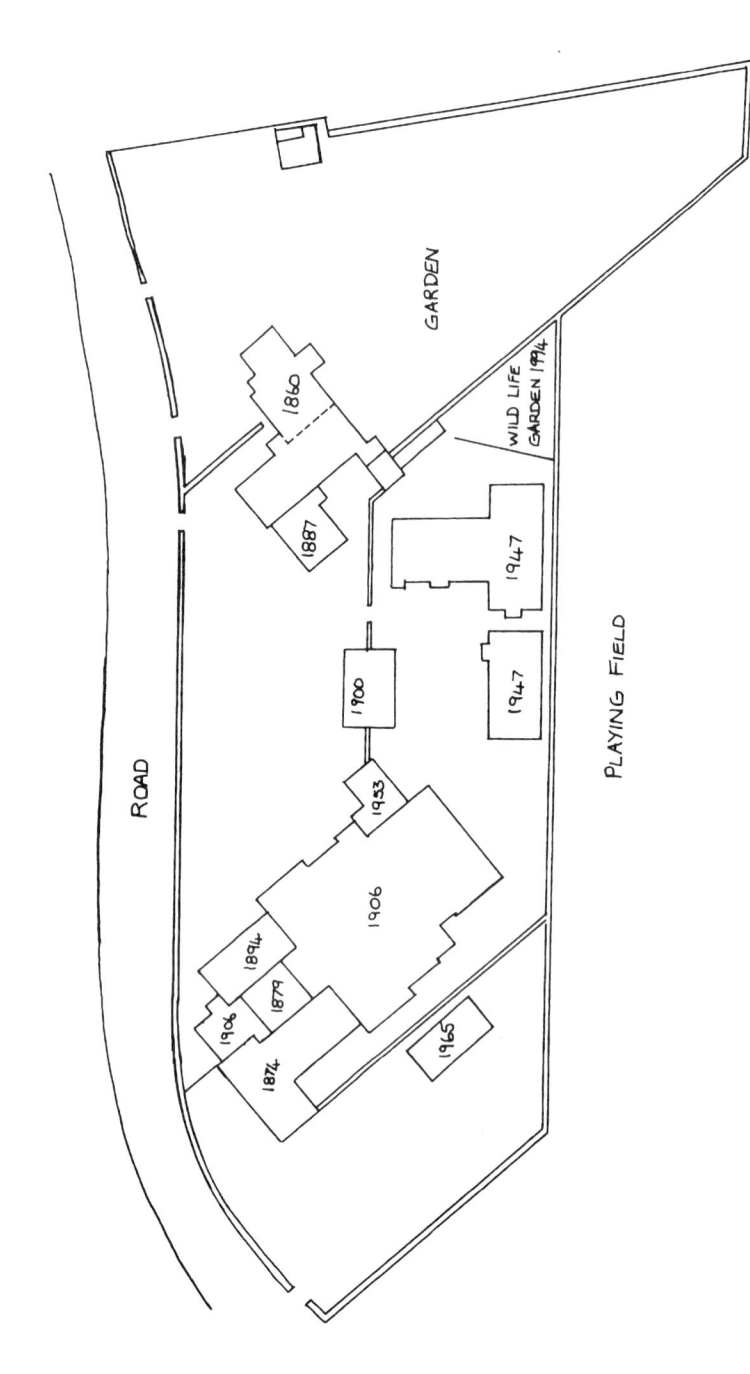

Plan of School Buildings 1860 – 1994

Kennay School 1905

A photograph taken from the Free Church Spire

School Board Members

The first School Board elected in Kemnay contained a reasonable cross section of members – both local ministers, Rev. George Peter of the Parish Church and Rev. J. Dymock of the Free Church, William Maitland who ran the general merchant's business in the Square and Alexander Moir, Kemnay Quarries. It was he who built Kaimhill Croft, off Aquithie Road, where he lived with his wife and family and his father. George Malcolm, farmer, Craigearn, whose family have been in the area for a long time, was also a Board member. Mr John Grant was appointed treasurer. He was a retired farmer in his seventies who lived in Birchfield, the house between High Street and Grove Road. Rev. George Peter served as Chairman to the Board. He came to Kemnay as minister in 1839 and remained until his death in 1898, at the age of 83 years. He was a bachelor all his life, his sister keeping house for him. Beloved by his flock, he was a fatherly figure about the area. Unlike many parishes in Scotland, the Disruption of 1843 made no difference in Kemnay, as George Peter remained with the Established Church.

It was not until the influx of people during the 1860's that a need was felt for a Free Church in the area. Rev. J. Dymock, the second minister, was ordained in 1870 and stayed until his death on February 4th 1899 at the age of 58 years. It was during his ministry that the Free Church building, now the Church Halls, was erected and opened for worship in 1873.

Many minutes handed down to us were quite sufficient at their time of writing, but as the years pass by and they are reread, we find that more information could have been provided. The members of the second School Board elected at Kemnay in 1876 consisted of Messrs Gellie, Moir, McCombie, Malcolm and the Rev. Peter. There is no doubt that at the time, these men would have been readily identified as they all were members of the same Board, but at this distance in time we have sometimes to make assumptions as to their identity, especially if there were several family members of the same name in the parish.

George Gellie was one of the early entrepreneurs in the village. He came as a young man to work in the quarries, and was at the time of his election to the School Board a superintendent there. He it was who took off the feu and built the property now occupied by the Gushet Neuk Bar. He then built

Albion in the High Street, where he was living at this time. This was followed by Woodbine, the house next door, and later on he built Gowanbank. Moir and Malcolm we must assume to be the two members from the previous Board, and McCombie we assume to be the tenant farmer of Milton who devoted sixty years of his life to public service, including nine years as convener of the County Council of Aberdeen. He died in March 1929, shortly before his eightieth birthday.

John Grant was dismissed, and in his place James Roy was appointed Clerk and Officer with Alex Whyte as Treasurer. James Roy resigned from his post on 14th July 1876 due to pressure of other commitments. Alex Whyte was appointed Clerk, a post which he was to hold until his death on 20th March 1924 at the age of 81 years. Like many of his generation, Alexander Whyte worked at the quarries where he was a journeyman mason and later a granite stone borer, or more commonly a driller. As we see above, he was appointed treasurer to the School Board and later clerk. He eventually built the house now known as Parkview, but then known as Bellaville, so named after his wife Annabella. As well as these appointments, he was also Inspector of the Poor and Collector of the Poor and other Rates. He was for a time Postmaster in the village. He built a wooden extension to the east side of his house which he called the office. It was here that the School Board sometimes met. His record of service to the community was considerable.

There is no mention of an Officer being appointed. The Minute of 30th April 1879 reads:

> Kemnay Public School. The first meeting of the new School Board was held here today. Present, Messrs Adam, Kendall Burnett, Christie and Gellie. Mr Gellie proposed that Mr Burnett of Kemnay be appointed Chairman of the Board. This was seconded by Mr Adam and unanimously agreed to. Mr Kendall Burnett was appointed Chairman pro tem.

W Kendall Burnett was a son of A G Burnett of Kemnay. He practised as a lawyer in Aberdeen and took considerable interest in the works of the School Board at Kemnay. He built 'The Grove' where he and his family stayed for a while. Following the death of Rev. George Peter, his sister moved to the Grove, where she lived until her death. Kendall Burnett died on July 17th 1912 at the relatively young age of fifty eight.

At the election of the Board in 1882, Christie was replaced by Warrack, who was for a time farmer at Scrapehard. George Gellie was appointed Chairman.

Whether or not his legalistic mind was at work we cannot say, but:
'The following code of rules were read by Mr Kendall Burnett and adopted.

1. No meeting of the Board shall be held on less than four clear days previous notice from the Clerk.
2. At meetings of the Board, the first business shall be the reading and approval of the minutes of the previous meeting. Thereafter, pieces of business left over from the previous meeting shall be proceeded with in the order in which they stand in the Minutes, thereafter, motions shall be discussed in the order in which the notices of them stand in the previous Minutes.
3. No member shall be entitled to propose a motion other than one directly arising from the discussion of a subject regularly before the Board, unless notice of it has been given at a previous meeting or unless written information of a motion to be proposed has been given to the Clerk in such time as to admit of his giving notice thereof to the members at least four clear days before the day of the meeting.
4. Any member taking part in a vote may at the same meeting enter his dissent from the resolution adopted, and either at that or the next following meeting give in reasons of dissent to be recorded in the Minutes, but no one who has not proposed a motion or recorded a vote on a matter under discussion shall have right to enter a dissent from a resolution of the Board, nor shall anyone be entitled to enter a dissent from any resolution except at the meeting at which it has been passed.'

The newly elected Board meeting for the first time on 28th April 1885 consisted of Messrs Kendall Burnett, Gellie, Melvin, Philip and Reid. Mr Kendall Burnett was unanimously elected Chairman. At this distance in time, it is difficult to identify with certainty the last three members.

At the meeting of 7th March 1887, we read: 'Mr Gellie having tendered his resignation as a member of the Board, owing to his having left the parish and gone to reside in the Island of Jersey.' An acknowledgement of his work for the Board was conveyed to Mr Gellie. He died in Aberdeen on

January 7th, 1905 at the age of sixty five years. Mr McCombie, Milton, Kemnay was unanimously appointed in his place.

A new Board met on 25th April, 1888 and the members were: Messrs W Kendall Burnett, James Halkett, George Milne, Andrew Petrie and George Robertson. James Halkett was a mason at the quarry, whilst Andrew Petrie carried on a general merchant's business at Donview Cottage which was on the site of the Burnett Arms Hotel. It was he who built the property now occupied by the Clydesdale Bank. Prior to his vacating Donview Cottage, Andrew Petrie was shrewd enough to apply for a hotel licence. The date on the bank property is 1888, and the architect for the project was Mr William Bremner of Alehousewells, who had recently taken a lease of that farm, he reputedly having been a surveyor on Fetternear estates. The Petries ran a general merchant's business in their new property. The frontage to the High Street consisted of the present chemist's shop front followed by the main shop front which had two large windows with a door between. This was the main entrance as the other door was mainly kept shut. The main shop consisted of two counters, the left hand being groceries and the right hand drapery, the smaller shop, now the chemist, housed the hardware and ironmongery, while beyond and behind the drapery, towards Station Road, was the china department. The bank agency was only a small area entered by the existing bank door on the corner. A dressmaking department existed downstairs.

The new Board meeting on 22nd April 1891 consisted of Messrs Kendall Burnett, W. Booth, J. Halkett, A. Petrie and J. Philip. Mr Burnett was unanimously returned to the chair.

The members certainly took their position seriously as we read in a minute of 10th January 1894: '…At this stage Mr Halkett stated that his daughter wished to become a candidate for the pupil teachership about to become vacant and in order that she might do so without prejudice handed in his resignation in writing to the clerk. The resignation having been accepted with expressions of regret Mr Halkett left the meeting.' His daughter was not appointed to the post, which was filled by Miss Christina Hardie.

On 2nd May 1894 the members of the newly elected Board were: Messrs W Kendall Burnett, Advocate, Aberdeen, Andrew Petrie, Bank Agent, Kemnay, Rev. A. Hood Smith, Kemnay, Peter Tawse, Birchfield, Kemnay and James Taylor, Aboyne Cottage, Kemnay. Rev. A. Hood Smith was ordained as assistant and successor to Rev. George Peter on 3rd May 1893. Mr Peter's health was by this time failing, but it must be remembered that he was a man aged 79 years and had been ministering to his flock in Kemnay for 54 years.

Over the years a number of the Board members had been men from the quarry, quite often from the managerial side. This time round was no different for we find Peter Tawse, a manager at the quarry a member. He was a member of the family which was to give their name to one of the well respected construction firms in the area, still retained in the name of Hall & Tawse. He died in 1907 at the age of 52. His son Bertram was one of the many from the village who gave their life during the First World War.

James Taylor was a mason at the quarry as well as being something of an entrepreneur. He built the property now known as Gordondale, followed by Aboyne Cottage, so called after the area where he was brought up, his parents staying at Ferrar, west of Aboyne. Later he built the house now known as Dunvegan, where he died in 1936.

1897 saw the return of Henry Durward McCombie in place of Peter Tawse. 1900 saw no change in the composition of the Board, but 1903 brought several changes as the Board elected that year consisted of Messrs George Bain, James Adam Diack, Henry Durward McCombie, Alexander Ogg and Rev. Alexander Hood Smith, who was unanimously elected Chairman.

George Bain, an Orkneyman, farmed at East Mains and Wellbush before returning to his native soil where he died at Saverock on April 27th, 1933 at the age of eighty eight. James Adam Diack was a son of one of the first families to come to the village at the outset of the quarries. He ran a tailor's business in the High Street where the hair stylist is now, and stayed in Benview, Kendall Road, which he built. He was the father of the noted educationalist and author, Hunter Diack. Alexander Ogg, who stayed in Laurelbank, Kendall Road, was an engineer at the quarry.

Rev. A. Hood Smith tendered his resignation as a member of the Board on June 10th 1904 prior to his departure to Newmachar. His place was filled by Alexander Sim Weir, Chemist, Blythewood, Kemnay, another business man of note in the community. The same members were re-elected in 1906.

Several changes took place in the Board elected in 1909. It consisted of Messrs John A. Burnett, John Diack, John Malcolm, Henry D. McCombie and A. S. Weir. John A. Burnett was the elder brother of Kendall Burnett and had succeeded to the estate of Kemnay on the death of his father A. G. Burnett the previous year. John Diack is difficult to place, but John Malcolm farmed at Craigearn and also practiced as a medical doctor in the parish. Mr McCombie was unanimously elected Chairman.

Alexander Sim Weir came to the village as chemist around the turn of the century. He stayed in Blythewood and his shop was in the High Street, now occupied by Lingard the butcher. He also performed dentistry as a sideline and took considerable interest in all aspects of village life.

The election of 1911 saw John Diack replaced by Rev. Andrew Downie, the parish minister. He was inducted in 1909 following the departure of Rev. P. G. Smith to Kippen. A bachelor, he was well loved by his flock in the village. His premature death in 1923 came as a shock to the community.

May 1914 saw several changes to the Board. This new Board consisted of John A. Burnett of Kemnay; James Dufton, Burnett Arms; Henry Durward McCombie, Milton; Dr. John Malcolm, Craigearn; Robert Petrie, Bank House; Alexander G. Reid, Gowanbank; Alexander S. Weir, Blythewood. John A. Burnett was appointed Chairman.

James Dufton was for a number of years publican at the Burnett Arms Hotel. Robert Petrie was a son of Andrew Petrie and served as Bank Agent in the village. Alexander G. Reid, along with his brother William Bisset Reid, ran a building firm in the village. A.G. as he was commonly called, so named after the previous laird of Kemnay, served on the Board for several years. He was for a long time parents' representative to the school.

This proved to be the last election of a School Board as the Minute of 15th May 1919 ends with:

> 'This being the last meeting prior to the Management being taken over by the new Authority the Chairman in bidding farewell to the members expressed the pleasure they all had in being able to hand over such a splendid building and such a fine staff of teachers'. (John A. Burnett, Chairman)

Extracts from the School Log Books (1873-1948)

Under the Education Act of 1872, headmasters were required to keep a log book of the significant events taking place in their school. Quite detailed instructions were laid down as to the type of subject matter to be noted and the manner in which it was to be recorded. The following was included in the 1873 Log Book as an example:

SPECIMENS OF SUCH WEEKLY ENTRIES.
As have been approved by H. M. Inspectors

March 21. School opened on Monday morning with praise and prayer. The Rev. Mr Milne, and Messrs Thomson, Arnott and Brown, School Board Members, were present to introduce as Head Teacher to the School, Mr Andrew Brodie, Certificated Second Class, from Free St Peter's Schools, Edinburgh, employed seven years in teaching. The most of the week has been occupied in understanding the arrangement of Classes, &c. Attendance fair. School opened and closed with prayer at the usual hours.

March 28. Attendance irregular this week, chiefly owing to bad weather. On Wednesday afternoon the II. and III. Standards had special drill in Arithmetic. Other Lessons according to Time Tables. Ordinary progress made.

April 4. Easter Week. Holidays.

April 11. Charles Ross, Pupil Teacher, absent on Thursday from sickness. A Monitor employed in his place. Commenced the Shorter Catechism in the Fourth Class this week. Lessons according to Time Tables. School opened and closed with prayer at the usual hours.

April 18. Attendance much better this week. Extra drill has been given this week in preparing for the Government Examination. Progress good. Visit from Mr Duff of the School Board on Friday afternoon, who waited until dismission. Nothing else worthy of remark.

SUGGESTIONS WORTHY OF NOTE.

The yearly date should be at the top of each page. The Log Book must be kept in School. One or two lines should be left as a space between each Entry. No special rule can be given as to the length of Entries, but three average Weekly Entries on a page have been accepted in England by Her Majesty's Inspectors. Personal opinions or reflections, such as "unpleasant visit from —— who gave me much impertinence," are not permitted, and may cause forfeiture of Certificate. Epidemics, fairs, &c., having influence in the attendance,– and new subjects or Books introduced should be noted.

Managers would do well to observe particularly Art. 17, e, of Scottish Code, which runs as follows: "Notice should be immediately given to the Department of the date at which the Teacher enters on the charge of the School, from which date the Grant is computed." By inattention to this the whole Grant, or portions thereof, have been frequently forfeited.

Article 37 of the Scottish Code reads 'No reflection or opinions of a general character are to be entered in the Log Book'. Consequently, much of the reading in the Kemnay Log Books is rather bland. On occasion, the reader can discern the emotions behind an entry and at times these do come bubbling up to the surface. For example, early on in these official records of the school, a battle of wills was developing between Miss Webster of the Girls' School and Mr Proctor, headmaster of the adjacent Parish school. Miss Webster's running complaint was that Proctor kept offloading boys and girls into her school, some of them above the agreed age of 7 and others of very limited educational abilities. The entry for 8th Dec. 1876 shows Miss Webster to be very distraught:

'My astonishment may be imagined to find the Master (Proctor) again admitting both boys and girls that have not passed the first Standard. And henceforth resolve never to come to terms of the kind again. If the Master admit children below Standard 1st, he must stand to the consequences. But I will never be again worried in like manner by the fickleness of Master, parent or child'.

Another example of a headmaster under extreme stress allowing emotional language to leech out onto the pages of the Log Book can be glimpsed when Mr Alexander in 1916 had the unenviable task of recording the toll of former pupils killed in the First World War. The entry for 8th December states:

'Work as usual: John Imlach, John Snowie, James Walker have fallen in the Great War: many have been murdered'.

The word 'murdered' has been erased by pen at a later date and the less emotive word 'killed' has been substituted.

The Log Books also deal with more mundane matters such as the weather. Extremes of heat and cold were guaranteed to get a mention if they affected the running of the school. Because pupils travelled to Kemnay from over 20 miles away, getting through to the school in bad winters could be a problem. Here are some entries from the early years of the school:

'Snow storm affected school attendance. On Wednesday, only 13 pupils present' (13th March 1874)

'Attendance meagre in last 3 days on account of tempestuous weather'. (22th October 1875)

'Monday and Tuesday very stormy days and the children could not come to school on account of the roads being blocked with snow. Miss Milne could not get here before 9 o'clock in the evening of Monday on account of the snowstorm and Miss Killoh did not arrive until Wednesday forenoon'. (3rd March 1893)

'Seventh week of snow began on Saturday last' (21st Dec. 1925)

Wintry weather also affected the internal workings of the school:

'Weather still stormy and intensely cold. Attendance very poor…No copy book writing done this week. Ink frozen and children too cold to write'. (21st Jan. 1881 – Girls' School Log)

Working in such conditions with little or no heating in the classroom must have been very unpleasant and it is little wonder that pupils were not turning up for lessons.

'The boiler in the cooking room grate has been destroyed by the frost and lessons are meantime stopped'. (1st Feb. 1918)

'Snowstorm and very severe frost over weekend. Furnace was left on, but let off for a short time on Saturday to allow plumbers to put in new bottom to furnace. Frost got into radiators, and one in Miss Argo's room burst on Sunday. Miss Gordon's room too had one frozen, which was thawed on Monday afternoon. The hot water cistern in cookery room also was frozen'. (19th Dec. 1927)

It is perhaps not surprising in Kemnay that mentions of extremely cold weather outweigh those for extremely hot conditions, but the latter do feature on occasion:

'Owing to excessive heat, many of children breaking down in health'. (18th July 1876)

'Heat excessive – longing much for holidays'. (25th July 1876)

Note that at this time, school went on until late July and the summer holidays were in August and early September. As the two following extracts show, teaching pupils in July was not a very productive exercise and by the mid-1920s, the modern pattern of holidays had come into being:

'The whole week has been very warm and lessons have not been on the whole well got up'. (24th June 1887)

'It is very warm meantime and some scholars show traces of being fagged out'. (13th July 1900)

Just as the school was often incapacitated due to the vagaries of the weather, so also outbreaks of contagious or infectious diseases could bring the school to its knees. For example, on 21st June 1878, the Log Book shows two cases of scarlet fever reported. On the following week, another incident was reported. On 4th October, the death of a little boy was recorded as a result of the fever which was still prevalent. Cases were reported up until January 1879 when it was said to have broken out at Kirkstyle. To compound this, on 25th July 1879, measles and whooping cough were reported to be prevalent and school attendance reduced. Teachers were not immune from catching whatever was going, especially as the classrooms were grossly overcrowded and ill-ventilated by modern standards. On 4th June 1880, Miss Godsman of the Infant Department was taken ill and it was subsequently found to be scarletina. As a result, the infants were dismissed for the rest of the week. The fever raged for some time and following consultation with the School Board, the school was closed for three weeks. On 9th July, the entry states that 'the Parish seems to be clear of Fever'.

Other infections which we take for granted these days could have serious consequences in the days before antibiotics and other medicines:

'A little boy Taylor has died this week from sore throat: and two or three others are reported as bad'. (24th April 1891)

The 'flu epidemic of the winter of 1918 decimated the whole of Europe. The virus swept the continent at the most inopportune time, with millions of people dislocated and starving. It is said that the pandemic killed more people than the carnage of the war itself. In Kemnay, the Log Book records the following:

'By order of Dr. Watt, Medical Officer for the County, the Elementary School has been closed owing to the recrudescence of influenza; the Higher Grade Department, not being affected, is to go on'. (6th Dec. 1918)

'Only Higher Grade Department in session this week. Influenza still rampant in the Parish'. (13th Dec. 1918)

'Attendance of Public School very low, cause of this is influenza which again rages in the parish: many deaths have occurred this week'. (14th Feb. 1919)

Other illnesses to strike at the pupils of Kemnay were measles and whooping cough. The Medical Officer closed the school due to an outbreak of measles in July 1895. Exactly a year later, whooping cough was the scourge and it is reported on 3rd July that 'considerably over 100 absent today'.

The reader of the Log Books can detect a decline in the incidence of mass epidemics affecting the work of the school. This was aided by the 1908 Education (Scotland) Act which made school medical inspection compulsory. We can see this in operation in the next extract:

'Dr. Sinclair examined a number of scholars medically; this was continued on Tuesday and Thursday when a lady dentist assisted him'. (25th Feb. 1921)

The Log Books faithfully record the coming and going of members of staff. On the whole, nothing out of the ordinary is to be found here. Only two entries are worthy of comment. Firstly, in 1896, the Log Book shows that there were 5 teachers on the Kemnay school roll, plus a pupil teacher, an ex-pupil teacher and a monitor. As the pupil roll in that year was 394, a quick calculation tells us that the average pupil-teacher ratio must have been about 60:1 i.e. nearly double the maximum class allowable nowadays!

The other entry worth mentioning concerns the departure of a respected teacher from Kemnay school:

'Next Friday, Miss L Adam gives up teaching. She has been long and honourably connected with the school, first as a pupil teacher, when she completed her apprenticeship by gaining by competition a first class in the list of entrants to the RC Training College. For a long period, she has taught Standard 4, now Senior 2 with the greatest acceptance and success. By her resignation, the school loses one of its best teachers. She is to be married'.

In these days before equal opportunities, women were not allowed to continue teaching after getting married. Whether Miss Adam gave up her post willingly is not known but clearly the school was the loser.

On more mundane matters, the Log Books record alterations to the fabric of the school and the introduction of new equipment. However, it has to be said that log books provide us with only a very incomplete picture of the fixtures and fittings of the building. Nevertheless, the fight to get better resources for the school was, and still is, a slow and frustrating process:

'Blackboard arrived today the need of which was intimated a year ago but it has got no stand and is of no more use than the bits of the old one we are using'. (20th Nov. 1874)

Other mention of new equipment is as follows:

- 1877 – received maps of Europe and Scotland
- 1882 – acquired piano and drill apparatus
- 1896 – mention of the use of a magic lantern for a Geography lesson
- 1909 – HMI report makes mention of a science laboratory and a woodwork workshop
- 1924 – new Principal Teacher of Modern Languages was treated to 'tea – speeches and selections on the school gramophone beguiled a pleasant two hours'. 1924 also saw the arrival of a new cyclostyle.

The Log Books contain their fair share of complaints and frustrations from the headmaster. Proctor arrived back after the summer vacation to find 'school has neither been plastered nor cleaned' (14th Sept. 1877). Another entry complains about the 'crowded state of Department. Average for week 100, as many as 105 having been present on one occasion, all requiring writing room'. (13th Jan. 1882)

On other occasions, the work of the school had to go on while alterations were being done to the building:

'Working conditions very unpleasant owing to building operations'. (25th May 1906)

'Work being done under great difficulties owing to so many classes being carried on in one room: attendance very good'. (11th July 1906)

Like all buildings, the school was subject to deterioration:

'Large piece of plaster fell from roof of woodwork room on Thursday'. (3rd Nov. 1922)

'Woodwork and cooking rooms declared unsafe'. (24th Nov. 1922)

'Cookery room roof oozing with water owing to washer in cistern overhead giving way from pressure of water during the weekend'. (27th Sept. 1927)

School Roll

Based on figures given in the log books, the roll of the school rose thus:

1878 – 93	1898 – 298	1912 – 460
1879 – 90	1899 – 361	1913 – 451
1886 – 120	1903 – 412	1914 – 405
1894 – 342	1904 – 380	1915 – 420
1895 – 300	1909 – 460	1918 – 396
1897 – 314	1911 – 451	1925 – 360

Subjects Taught

Log books are also useful for finding out what subjects were taught at various times in the past. In the early log books, mention is made of Singing, Latin, Reading, Arithmetic, Dictation, Sewing, Cookery. A Cookery class was begun on Monday 10th of June 1889 by Miss Black. A class for adults met on Monday, Wednesday and Friday and for young girls on Tuesday, Thursday and Saturday. The entry for June 1896 states leaving certificate exams being conducted at Kemnay were Arithmetic, Geometry, Algebra, English, French and Latin. The following year, mention is given of Mathematics and Greek being taught. The Log Books show that Kemnay had Science and Art Departments by 1898. The teaching of Drawing was started on 16th March 1900. HM Inspectors attended the school on 30th October 1908 and gave orders for the teaching of woodwork. This was duly started in November. In August of the next year, mention is made of a Manual Instruction workshop at the school. Laundry was also added to the curriculum that session.

Prior to the war, concern had been raised about the 'physical deterioration' of the people of Britain. The Liberal Government passed legislation to guarantee the provision of school medical inspection and school meals. With the war looming, physical education (as we now call it) was looked at by the school inspectors. The Log Books mention that physical exercise was inspected by the HMI in 1913. The following year, PE was considered by the inspectors to be 'good as far as it goes but (exercises) should be made much more stimulating and vigorous and should be performed with greater precision'. In 1921, the HM report on physical training at Kemnay stated that 'a visiting expert has just been appointed and the PT is being reorganised throughout the school. The children are very responsive'. In 1919, the County Education Authority laid down regulations that 'religions' were now to be taught.

School Closure

The Headmasters of schools at this time had a lot more freedom to determine the educational experience of their pupils. This comes out quite clearly when looking at reasons given in the Log Books for closing the school:

'On account of the review of the volunteers at Nether Mains, a holiday had to be given today'. (26th June 1885)

'Wombwell's Menagerie was in the Village on Wednesday and a half holiday was given in order that the children might see the show'. (17th July 1891)

'Wednesday being day of Rev. A. Hood Smith's induction as Minister of the Parish, was observed as a holiday throughout the Parish'. (5th May 1893)

'Tomorrow fixed for school treat and so no school'. (29th Aug. 1895)

'School closed out of respect to the memory of Rev. Mr Peter, minister of the parish'. (16th Dec. 1897)

'Midday interval lengthened to allow the pupils to see an army biplane which had alighted in a field near the school'. (4th Apr. 1913)

'Scholars given permission to view the eclipse; it was cloudless and a fine view was obtained'. (8th March 1921)

There were other times when pupils took time off school without gaining permission. Some of the attractions pulling pupils away from the seat of learning would not arouse the modern pupil's interest in the slightest:

'Attendance on Friday was thinner than usual on account of 2 travelling threshing mills being in the neighbourhood' (21st Dec. 1877)

'Thursday 6th being the day of two displenish Sales in the Parish, the School was more thinly attended than usual'. (7th May 1880)

Pupils benefited from school closures for other reasons, many of them to do with Royalty, which in those days was held in very high esteem:

Holidays were given for Queen Victoria's Diamond Jubilee on 22nd June 1897; the funeral of Edward VII on 20th May 1910; royal weddings in March 1922 and April 1923; a visit of the King and Queen to Aberdeen to open the Art Gallery Extension on 29th Sept. 1925.

Other national events did now and again intrude and make the pupils' attempts to get to school more difficult than normal. For example, the 1919 national railway strike gets a mention:

'Much dislocation of work might have occurred this week owing to Railway Strike but pupils from long distances – Alford and beyond – have shown a fine spirit and have rarely been absent'. (3rd Oct. 1919)

The same determination and initiative to get to school is also found during the General Strike of 1926:

'From Tuesday of this week, pupils coming by train have felt the inconvenience of the General Strike, but Jaffray's 'bus has been a great boon at this time, and the train pupils have made exemplary attendance, most availing themselves of the 'bus, some even cycling the twenty odd miles. For many of the pupils, it has meant leaving home before 7a.m. and not reaching home till 8 p.m. or later' (7th May 1926)

Miscellaneous log book entries 1928-48

June 27 1928: Twenty eight certificates were awarded for perfect attendance, and Kathleen Marriott, who had completed six years of perfect attendance received the Authority's special prize of 10/- in books. Robina Bruce also had 6 years, but not consecutive.

Sept 14 1928: A week of lovely sunshine, compensating for the dreadful rain of previous weeks.

Sep 26 1928: This was the first day of the Games Period for Secondary Department. The last period of Wednesday afternoon has been curtailed to 40 minutes instead of 65 minutes, the 2.50 - 3pm interval being dropped, and the Secondary Dept dismissing at 3.30, to go to

Playing Field for 45 minutes of organized games. Hockey was inaugurated this afternoon under the tuition of Mr Shand and Miss Henderson. Mr Gall supervised the football, and Miss Ogilvie the Netball. All the pupils took part in the games and seemed to enjoy themselves.

April 12 1929 Friday: This evening, and on Saturday forenoon the Halls were hung with pictures taken from 'Pictorial Education', and mounted and framed by Mr George Cruickshank, Kemnay. The cost is £15 or thereby, and is met from the Schol Activities Fund.

June 4 1929 Tuesday: Parts were allocated today for the Annual Open Air Shakespeare play. This year we are to do 'Twelfth Night', this day three weeks.

Dec. 2 1929: The busts loaned by Sir Arthur Grant of Monymusk House are now placed in the Hall on ledges above the various classroom doors, also a statue of Sir Walter Scott presented by Mrs Petrie, senr., The Bankhouse Kemnay. Mrs Petrie has also presented the school with a fine flagpole.

Dec. 7 1929: John McKenzie, Janitor, went today to Aberdeen Royal Infirmary for an operation for appendicitis. His work is being done by Edward Ross.

Dec. 24 1929. John McKenzie, Janitor, died this morning at one o' clock in the Royal Infirmary. There had been a second operation and he never recovered his strength.

Mr McKenzie was the first full time janitor of this school, and he entered into the activities of the school with great zest. Trained as a joiner he was the ideal handy man, and he has left many memorials of his handiwork in the school. The new bookcase to which he put the finishing touch the very day he left for the Infirmary is to be called after him the McKenzie Bookcase. In our school concerts and plays he was an enthusiastic worker, and the platform and trestles which we use in the Hall were put together by him last summer.

Feb. 21 1930: This has been a week of snow and frost, the first this winter, which has been exceptionally open. School has been free from epidemics, and the attendance in both departments has been very good. It was 98.1 for the Secondary Department, the last five weeks, counting up to last Friday 14th February.

April 11 1930: School closed this afternoon for the Easter Vacation to resume Tuesday 22nd instant. To conclude the afternoon the Headmaster gave a brief description of his voyage last summer to the Mediterranean to the assembled school.

April 23 1930: At SMC meeting today Mr Edward Ross was recommended for the post of Janitor of this school out of ten applicants.

June 27 1930: Prizegiving: …For perfect attendance there were 73 certificates awarded, a record number for the school. Two pupils have completed a wonderful record—Lily W Forbes, Bridgeview, 6 years consecutive of perfect attendance, and Violet W Laing, Breda, Alford, 10 years. The latter is also dux of the school. George W Lawrie is dux of the intermediate school.

Oct. 8 1930: A Continuation Class in Singing has been formed under Mr Green, and practices have begun for an operetta.

Dec. 5 1930: This is the most serious epidemic (measles) since I came to this school. The percentage of attendance in the Infants and Primary I for the week is as follows:

Monday 50%; Tuesday 43.7; Wed 32.5; Thursday 26.2; Friday 18.7; week 34.2%. Today, Friday, there are just six infants in school, 1 junior, 5 senior. The roll of Infants and Primary 1 is 80.

Feb. 20 1931: This afternoon the Headmaster attended the funeral of Mrs Dufton, Burnett Arms Hotel, a lady who showed much kindness to the School, helping with a quiet, unostentatious generosity.

March 6 1931: The snow has lain all the week; there has been severe frost, the temperature being below zero one day in Kintore. Today more snow has fallen. The attendance is very poor in consequence of the storm and the prevalent influenza. There are over 60 pupils absent in the Primary School.

March 25 1931: The evening class in Singing under Mr Green is presenting the Operetta "The King of Kandy" tonight in Public Hall, Kemnay, also Friday and Saturday evenings.

April 2 1931: Mr Green absent today with illness.

May 22 1931: Mr Green, Singing Master, died at his home, 7 Westfield Gardens, Inverurie, this evening. It is just two months since he conducted his successful operetta "The King of Kandy", 27th and 28th March.

Among the pictures which hung in Kemnay School for many years was one of the cast of The King of Kandy. It was taken after the death of Mr Green, but the photographer added a picture of Mr Green seated at the bottom right hand corner of the picture.

June 26 1931: Prizegiving: The ceremony took place in the afternoon in the School Hall, at half past two o' clock, the chair being taken by A S Weir Esq, Blythewood, Kemnay,who in the course of the past session severed a long connection with the school, having been one of the main promoters of the original Higher Grade School, and having held office as local member of S.M.C., Clerk, and again member of the new area Alford S.M.C.

The prizes were presented by Mrs Weir, and Mr Weir, in the course of his reminiscent remarks, made the generous offer to the school of a mural tablet to be placed in the Hall, recording the names of the School Duxes since the year when prizes were first given in the school.

July 1 1932: The Annual Prize Giving was held in the School this afternoon ...and a notable item in the proceedings was the unveiling of a handsome panel in oak commemorating the Duxes of the school from the year 1916. This gift was presented by A S Weir, Esq, Blythewood, Kemnay who has been for so many years identified with the interests of the school both as member of the School Board, Education Authority, and lately as Clerk to the School Management Comittee. The panel, which is in perfect harmony with the War Memorial, makes a handsome addition to the already beautiful School Hall.

June 30 1933: Prize Giving: This was the first occasion on which the Miss Yeats Prize for Dux of the Primary School was awarded, and the winner was Andrew Mathieson, whose family has now gone to a farm in Yorkshire. The other prize, endowed by Miss Yeats, awarded to the pupil making most progress in Class V of Primary School was won by Anna Sybil Moir.

April 27 1934: The school enjoyed a visit this forenoon from its old and esteemed Qualifying Mistress, Miss Yeats, who is at present on holiday in Aberdeen.

August 22 1934: This evening at a public meeting of parents of the parish, Mr Robert Chivas, Nether Inver, Monymusk, member of the Education Committee presiding, A. G. Reid, Esq, The Knowe, Kemnay, was proposed as parents' representative in room of the late Rev. J W Jackson, on the nomination of James Philip, farmer, Sunnyside, seconded by George Clark, settmaker, Star House, Kemnay, these being the only two parents present besides the Headmaster and the Janitor. There being no other nomination Mr Reid was declared elected. Mr Reid was once a member of the Kemnay School Management Committee.

Jan. 28 1935: ...The big item of news this morning was the success of Violet Connon, Primary IV in the 'Ovaltine' Essay Competition. She is first in her division for the best composition written by a girl under 11 on the theme: " 'Ovaltine' What it is and what it does." The competition was open to all Primary Schools or Primary Divisions of Schools in Aberdeen, Banff, Kincardine, Moray and Nairn. Mr Maurice James, the adjudicator, writing to announce the result, speaks of Violet as, "vanquishing thousands of the competitors." He asks for a little function for the presentation of the prize on Tuesday afternoon, 9th February at 3 o' clock The prize is a magnificient one – "The Book of Knowledge" in 8 volumes. (Sold at £6. 2. 6d) The whole school rejoices in Violet's success.

April 26 1935: Dr. Riddoch, retired rector of Mackie Academy, Stonehaven, visited the school today to examine the LC candidates in Latin and Greek...

Ella Gall, a candidate for lower Latin, was absent at Aberdeen, competing in the Piano Solo section of Music Festival, and had to be sent for by car to submit to the oral examination as her work in Latin was 'doubtful.' ...Ella Gall left immediately after the oral examination, returned to Aberdeen, took part in another piano solo competition, was first and won the Challenge Silver Cup in her division, thus bringing a crowded day to a very successful conclusion.

June 26 1936: Prize Giving: ...The Primary Dux is Violet S Connon, who wins the Miss Yeats Prize. The Intermediate Dux is Isabella Thomson, and the Dux of the School is Jean McGregor Edwards, who is only 16 years of age and who has received her entire education at this school. She has done remarkably well in the Leaving Certificate Examination, winning it with 4 Highers and a lower at one sitting, all before she is 17. Her passes are English, H. French, H. Latin, H. Mathematics and L. German. She is to return to school another year and prepare for the Bursary Competition in Arts and Medicine.

No pupil leaves this year for the University.

August 17 1936: ...Certain Classrooms have been painted during the holidays, and as usual the Janitor, Mr Edward Ross, has the entire buildings and rooms in splendid order.

August 21 1936: The Milk in Schools Scheme is to be started in this school, beginning Monday 24th instant, under the auspices of the Aberdeen and District Milk Marketing Board. Supplies of milk are to come from the Home Farm at Monymusk, of which Mr E J Bremner, Beech Lodge, Monymusk is Manager. Up to Friday 123 pupils in Primary and Secondary Departments have signified their willingness to take milk so provided at ½d a third of a pint, pasteurised Grade 'A' (T.T.).

October 1 1936: The Headmaster sent for three boys who were being employed potato gathering at Nether Coullie by Mr Robert Connon. The boys all reported back to school before midday.

Dec. 23 1936: ...The usual Xmas concert was held in the afternoon. Apart from the usual items the most notable event was the first public appearance of the School Orchestra – twenty violins – under the leadership of Mr John Morgan, B.B.C. who is a former pupil of the school. The collection, which was a silver one, amounted to £4.10.6d...The remaining 10s is to be spent in providing a Xmas Box for the family of Duncan, Cairnton, every member of which, from parents to newborn babe, has had scarlet fever.

An epidemic of influenza had been affecting attendances all the month of January.

Feb.1 1937: This has been the worst attendance yet – 132 absentees, almost half the school. There was a severe snowstorm over the weekend, changing to rain on Sunday morning. Many roads are blocked, and cars and 'buses are stranded.

March 12 1937: This morning's newspaper contained the announcement of the sudden death of Miss Yeats, formerly Mistress of the Qualifying Class, at her home, 1 Little Road, Liberton, Edinburgh on Thursday 11th instant. On the 15th of this month it will be exactly five years since Miss Yeats was absent from school, and a day or two later tendered her resignation. ...prayer was offered for the beautiful memory and example left to teachers and pupils alike by one who had taught two generations of Kemnay scholars, and the Headmaster once more paid tribute to the life and character, the work and faithfulness of a teacher who gave her whole teaching career in this one school – 37 years.

Sept. 15 1937: The death, very suddenly, of Rev. Robert Keltie, M.A. at the Manse, Humbie, is reported in this morning's paper. The Headmaster alluded after morning prayers to the sad announcement of the passing of the former parish minister of Kemnay, recalling his energetic work for the renovation of the old parish church, his love of Kemnay, and his kindliness to all the children; and expressing the deep sympathy of the school with the widow, brother and the children, all of whom had at one time been pupils of this school.

Comment made by the Headmaster after almost a month of severe stormy weather:

Dec. 25 1937: The roads are clear at last and the good brown earth is visible once more. The sun is shining today, as if with youthful strength. Attendances for the month have been much below normal owing to the mumps and the storm.

Jan. 17 1938: Today the new Electric Light installation was inaugurated.

Jan. 28 1938: Today the Pye School Receiving Radio was inaugurated in the Hall in the afternoon in the presence of the assembled school. ...The set, which has been provided from our own School Activities Fund, has been purchased from Mr Mackie, Inverurie, who has installed the Electric power in the school.

March 16 1938: This evening in the Public Hall the united school orchestras of Kemnay Secondary School, Kintore Higher Grade School and Monymusk Public School gave their first combined performance in public to a hall that was packed out at the door, under the talented leadership of a former pupil of this school, Mr John Morgan, now a well known artist of the B.B.C.

It is a matter of only two years since the first set of violins was purchased and practice begun from the foundation. All agreed that the fifty two violins gave a marvellous performance for the time they had been under tuition.

May 4 1938: Dr. Macleod HMIS visited school this morning. ...He expressed his pleasure at the school having a Radio set of its own, and also the fine pictures in Hall and classrooms. It was a notable achievement, he said, to have a school doing so much "from within".

June 21 1938: The first two performances of the annual Open Air Shakespeare Play were given this afternoon and evening under the old beech tree at Kemnay House. This year the play chosen was "The Two Gentlemen of Verona" and Miss Henderson, as in former years, cooperated with the Headmaster in producing the play. The afternoon performance was meant specially for schools, and by permission of HMCIS and the Director the attendance of pupils at the play was allowed as a school attendance. Parties of pupils attended accordingly from as far as Corgarff, Strathdon and Rhynie, and the Demonstration School, Aberdeen.

Wind affected the hearing of the afternoon performance, but the conditions were much more favourable in the evening when the North Aberdeen Unionist Association attended to the number of 143, accompanied by Mr and Mrs Burnett of Powis.

Sept. 29 1938: This afternoon a Mrs Pimm from London, a medical doctor and the wife of a doctor, called at school in a state of agitation to ask if one of her children, whom she had brought from London in the present state of alarm for air-raids if war broke out, might attend school here in the meantime. The boy who is six years of age has been enrolled accordingly.

Oct. 18 1938: The London pupil, David Pimm, has left school to return to his home in London. It transpires that the boy's great grandfather and a great uncle were both boarders at this school in the middle of last century when the school was called Kemnay Academy and received boarders.

June 15 1939: Word has come today of the death last night at 11 o' clock of a pupil in the Senior Infants, Irene Gordon, Lachshellach. Irene was one of the brightest and happiest of children, and it is only three weeks since she left home to go to the Sick Children's Hospital for glandular trouble. She was a leading actor in our Braid Scots Concert in February, and both in day school and Sunday School she was a little ray of sunshine. Her classmates, the Infant Teachers and the Headmaster have sent a wreath.

Feb. 6 1940: The snow has lain on the ground since before the New Year, so there have been six weeks of severe winter conditions, during part of which time the Don has been frozen. The frost is being compared with that of 1894.

Aug. 23 1940: First prize in her section of Ovaltine Essay Competition is Ethel Jane Weir who receives her award of the Book of Knowledge: eight volumes valued at £6. 2s 6d. (p132)

Oct. 15 1940: Word has come today to Mr Baillie to report for military service in the Royal Artillery, at Bude, Cornwall, on Tuesday 22nd instant. He has asked to be released from duty as from Wednesday evening after concluding his Men's Keep Fit Class as he wishes to go home to Brora before joining up.

Presentation of Prizes for the Ovaltine Essay Competition

Among those included in the photograph are Jean Rose, Mr J Minto Robertson, Ann Morgan, Hilda Brown, Ann Harvey, James Cruickshank, James McDonald, Ethel Weir, Robert Moir and Francis Scollay.

Oct. 29 1940: Word has come to Mr Clark, Classical Master, to report for military service at Chelsea, London, to join the Scots Guards on Thursday 7th November.

Oct. 8 1941: One Hundred Years Ago. Aberdeen Journal. Price 4½d Wed. Oct 6 1941 No. 4891. School of Kemnay. We observe that the well known parochial school of Kemnay is about to be reopened after the harvest vacation. The example set by Mr Stevenson is one which has justly excited the attention of observers in all parts of the country, as almost the first instance of a parish school becoming invested with the merits of a boarding academy. Dickens has explored the best of the Yorkshire schools. He has blown up Do-the-boys Hall. It ought to be known, however, that an excellent education with every security for kind and benevolent treatment for the pupils, can be had at Mr Stevenson's seminary, for a sum as low as that charged by the Yorkshire schoolmasters.

The above quoted extract is from the Aberdeen Press & Journal of Tuesday 7th October 1941 and is singularly apropos of our schools closing this summer to suit harvest. History repeats itself.

Jan. 26 1942: When school met at 10 o' clock this morning there were 29 pupils present in the Secondary Division and 47 in the Primary. Eight teachers were absent, namely Miss Argo and Miss Fraser in Primary Department, and Misses Henderson, Robertson, Mitchell, Leslie, Reid and Mr Duncan in Secondary. The teachers present were – Miss Bremner, Miss Harper, Miss Gordon in Primary, Miss Melvin, Mr Gall in Secondary, and the Headmaster. This is the third of successive severe winters and it is the worst within memory.

Tuesday Jan. 27 1942: Miss Henderson, English Mistress, whose home is in Banchory, left there on Sunday morning, stayed overnight in Imperial Hotel, came by train to Kintore Monday forenoon and walked from there to Kemnay, arriving in Kemnay at 3 o' clock in afternoon. She is on duty this morning.

Miss Argo, Infants and Primary I, and Miss Robertson, Geography and assistant in mathematics, reported for duty at 11.30 this forenoon, having walked together from Kintore this forenoon, taking two and a half hours to the journey.

February 5 1942: Still no transport, mail or newspapers.

February 9 1942: The train service has resumed on Kintore – Alford line, and Alford pupils have come by train accordingly.

Feb 16 1942 Monday: Bus transport has resumed since Sunday.

March 25 1942: Mr Ian Simpson, M.A. Principal Teacher of English, Hermitage School, Helensburgh, a native of Monymusk, where his father was schoolmaster, has won the E.I.S. Prize Essay to Graduates for the best history of a parish school – in this case, Kemnay. He has very kindly presented the essay to the School Library. The history of the school goes back to 1600.

March 26 1942: The Headmaster received a telegram at noon today announcing the death of the former headmaster, Mr William Alexander at his home in Stirling this morning. It is nineteen years this June since Mr Alexander retired at the age of 62. He broke his leg a fortnight ago when he went outside to see if the black-out was right, and he has been more or less unconscious since the accident. Otherwise he was still vigorous and in the enjoyment of good health. He was the creator of Kemnay Secondary School and gave the best years of his life to the promotion of the school and the welfare of the pupils. In the words of Hamlet, 'He was a man, Take him for all in all, We shall not look on his like again.'

July 2 1943: Prize Giving: ...The Headmaster gave his usual report, commenting on the extended activities of school-teaching as now carried on, and explaining once more how the fact there was a prize-giving at all was entirely due to the money raised by the Shakespeare play, which in addition kept all the school activities going.

The new Dux prize has been presented by Dr. and Mrs Gordon Davidson, Grimsby, and is of the value of three guineas. In a letter announcing the prize to the Headmaster Dr. Davidson, who is himself an enthusiastic student and lover of Shakespeare wrote as follows: "This gift is prompted largely by our admiration of the good work done in the Kemnay School as judged by the records of its former pupils, and partly by special prominence which is given to the study of Shakespeare. The widespread interest in Aberdeenshire in the annual play under the beech trees speaks volumes for the individuality of the school, and of the staff. The pupils are indeed fortunate in having presented to them in so stimulating a manner a study which is at once of the highest educational value and a continual source of enjoyment and interest in after life."

The prize is to be known as "The Gordon Davidson Prize", and, appropriate enough, in accordance with the sentiments expressed by the Donor of the Prize, the first Dux to win the prize played the leading part in this year's Shakespeare Play, namely, John G M Robertson, who was "Macbeth".

Jan. 19 1945: The snowstorm and severe frost following have caused great havoc in telegraph wires and poles, blocking trains. There is a complete cessation of communication with the outside world by road, rail, mail, telephone, telegraph, newspapers. All electric power is cut off. There are 121 absentees in Primary department, and 54 in Secondary. Infants had a 'double' attendance, dismissing at 1pm. The following members of staff were unable to reach school: Miss Mitchell, visiting teacher of art, Miss N Reid, visiting teacher of domestic science, Miss Jessie Reid, physical instructress, and Miss Robertson, assistant in mathematics who travels daily from Kintore.

Jan. 22 1945 Monday: Electric power was restored on Saturday evening.

Newspapers and mails resumed this morning with the reopening of railway service. No buses running as yet, and telephones are still dead.

All the members of staff were present today except Miss Mitchell, who is ill, and Miss Jessie Reid, who is due here in afternoon and who has probably stayed the whole day at Alford P. School. Primary absences today are 90, and Secondary 38. The frost is still severe, and more snow fell at the weekend. The road is still blocked at Whitehouse.

Jan. 29 1945 Monday: There has been more snow over the weekend, and the fall of snow is considered greater than in January 1942. Trains are running, but there has been no 'bus service since Thursday afternoon a week past. The frost this storm is considered the worst since 1895.

Jan. 30 1945: A heavy fall of snow overnight, seven inches deep. Trains held up, three teachers, Miss Roberston, from Kintore, Miss N Reid from Aberdeen, and Mr Chalmers, visiting teacher of Benchwork from Kintore, not arriving till 11 am.

Pupils were allowed off by Headmaster to distribute newspapers. Two boys from Secondary Department have been taking the postal round of one of the postmen who is ill.

March 7 1945: The announcement of the conferring of the Honorary Degree of LLD on the Headmaster of this School by the Senatus Academicus of Aberdeen University, his own Alma Mater, appeared in the Stop Press News of Aberdeen Evening Express.

April 9 1945: Word has come from the Director that the Scottish Education Department is prepared to allow Miss Jeannie Bremner to continue in teaching service until the end of Session 1945-46. Miss Bremner was due to retire on 2nd June, but owing to the shortage of teachers the Director has asked her to continue meantime.

April 24 1945: Gladys Walker, a pupil of Class VI in Secondary Department, has been asked by Miss Elizabeth Adair of the Aberdeen BBC to take part in a Scots programme on Wednesday, May 9th by singing some Scots songs.

April 30 1945: Wintry weather has set in again – 'the teuchats' storm' or else 'the gab o' May'. The ground was white in the morning, and there have been heavy showers of snow all day.

The film 'The Mount Everest Expedition', the official film of the 1933 expedition, led by Mr Hugh Routledge, was shown this forenoon at 10 o' clock to the whole school in the Hall. By a fortunate coincidence a member of a former Everest expedition, Dr. Longstaff, is at present resident in Kemnay for the fishing season; and the Headmaster, through the friendly medium of Mr Lawson, another angler, was able to get Dr. Longstaff to address the school and also give a most interesting running commentary on the film. Dr. Longstaff was accompanied by his wife and Mr Lawson and another angler from the hotel.

August 2nd 1945: This forenoon Mrs Smart, (nee Netta Terras Gordon) a former pupil of this school visited the Headmaster. Mrs Smart was first bursar in 1901 at Aberdeen University Arts Bursary Competition – the first lady bursar in the history of the University – at the age of 15½ years. She was a pupil of this school her entire school career, which was under the late Mr Alexander. She and the present Headmaster were at college together and took Hons. Classics together.

Jan. 9 1946: Operations have begun in connection with the Dining Hall and Kitchen to be erected in the Boys' Playground.

Feb. 21 1946: A former pupil and Dux of the school Hunter Diack did a BBC broadcast this evening in the series, "Aberdeen Awa", with granite for his theme, and Kemnay as the background to his Anthology. Thus the School has figured in two of these Broadcasts.

March 15 1946: Word has come from the Director this morning that Mr Donald J. Baillie, who has been on military service, intends to resume duty here on Tuesday 26th instant, so replacing Miss Nellie A. Robertson, M.A. Also, Mr Norman W. McN. Clark, classical master, is to resume duty on Tuesday 23rd April, so replacing Mr Walter Duncan who goes on that date to Peterhead Academy as classical assistant. Miss Robertson is to take up a temporary post for the summer term in Turriff Secondary School as assistant in Mathematics and Science.

March 21 1946: Councillor A. Fraser MacIntosh and Mr Alex McBean, Superintendent of Public Parks, visited the Headmaster this forenoon to ask for an Open Air Shakespeare Performance in one of the City Parks this summer. The agreement reached was for a repeat performance of whatever play the school did this summer a week later than the Kemnay performance, Wednesday June 19th and 26th being the respective dates.

April 3 1946: A School Service for Passiontide was conducted in the School Hall this forenoon 11.00 to noon by Rev. John Shand M.A. of

St Anne's Episcopal Church. The Primary Choir sang Katherine Tynan's "All in an April Evening", and a group of pupils read the Lesson from St John's Gospel, "I am the Good Shepherd". Mr Shand's address was on Christ as the Lamb of God.

April 4 1946: Acknowledgement has come of the collection taken for the Scottish fund for the children of Greece at the recent Ministry of Information Film in the School Hall amounting to £1. 8s. In reply to the Headmaster's Greek quotation the Hon Secretary, Mrs Helene Tombagis replied in Greek, but alas! modern Greek.

June 4 1946: Mrs Cruickshank and Miss Gordon left school this afternoon at 2.30 to set out for London by train from Aberdeen to attend the Garden Party in Buckingham Palace Grounds on Thursday, 6th June for representatives of the National Savings Committees. They will be absent till Monday, 10th June.

Sept. 13 1946: Today the first sale of school jam was held, beginning from Infant Department. The sale amounted to £6. 3s, and this sum has been added to the School Activities Fund Account in North Bank, Kemnay.

The collection of Rose Hips, under the supervision of Miss Gordon, continues with enthusiasm.

Oct. 1 1946: The old Hot Dinner scheme was recommenced today pending the inauguration of the new school canteen.

Jan. 6 1947: Owing to the shortage of Domestic Science teachers, and the prolonged absence of Miss Meta R G Forbes, who is now in a military hospital undergoing treatment for Diabetes, it has been impossible to fill the vacancy in the usual way, and as a temporary measure Miss C S Gordon, teacher of Primary V, who has certain D S qualifications under Article 55, has gallantly consented to take on the whole work of the Department, including the putting forward of three candidates for Lower Domestic Science in the Senior Leaving Certificate Examination.

With equal gallantry Mr George Copland M.A., retired schoolmaster of Auchterless P.S., now resident at Loanend, Kemnay, has consented to take the Qualifying Class. This is the twelfth school Mr Copland has done service in since he retired.

Feb. 10 1947: The snowstorm has come to Scotland now, and the Alford connection is cut owing to a lorry that has stuck in a snow wreath and blocked all 'bus traffic.

The absentees in primary are 82, in Secondary 47.

Feb. 28, Friday: Snow fell again heavily overnight. No vehicles on road or rail. The attendance for the week has been remarkable – 78% in both Divisions.

March 10 1947: This is the sixth week of the snow storm, which shows no sign of a thaw. The frost held all last week.

Miss MacGlashan HMI examined the three candidates in Domestic Science and expressed herself very well pleased with their attainments. The difference in the Cookery Room she described as 'unbelievable', and again she said 'The Domestic Science Department has come alive again.'

March 17 1947. Monday: This is now the seventh week of the snowstorm. On Sunday a thaw set in with the result that roads were impossible for vehicles. Attendance is still remarkably good.

March 26 1947: The snow is at last going and we see the earth again with a sense of relief and gladness. The only eyesore is the playground, which is really little better than a quagmire.

August 19 1947: This has been the most remarkable summer we have had for years. No-one remembers anything like it. Both July and August have been without rain, and the sunshine has been almost tropical. It continues still.

March 22 1948: Messrs Peterkin & Duncan, Advocates, 21 Golden Square Aberdeen, have allocated £20 to this school for the purchase of books in religious instruction from Mr Robert Donaldson's Trust. This method of encouraging Bible Knowledge has been substituted for the former method of Annual Competition, in which this school took so creditable a share. A selection of suitable literature has been suggested by Dr. Rusk, Lecturer in Bible, Aberdeen Training Centre, and from that list the Headmaster has made his own choice. The first consignment of books came this weekend to the amount of £7 1s 9d. The rest chosen are meantime out of print or reprinting and will be supplied when available.

March 23 1948: Word has come this morning of the re-grading of this school as providing education for pupils of age from 5 to 15 years. A modifying scheme embodying this amendment has been submitted for the approval of the Secretary of State. The Committee have agreed that pupils in the present fourth and/or subsequent years of the Secondary Course shall have the option of completing the Senior Leaving Certificate at Kemnay, or of transferring to Inverurie Academy at the commencement of session 1948–49. Pupils in the present third year class who do not intend to proceed to a Senior Leaving Certificate Course (at Inverurie) may be enrolled in a fourth year course at Kemnay.

Pupils at present in attendance at Kemnay who will transfer to Inverurie next session and whose homes are in excess of the appropriate statutory walking distance from the Academy there will be eligible to apply for travelling facilities, for which completed forms of application should be forwarded to the Director well before the end of the session.

This brings to an end the status of this school as a Senior Secondary School at the close of this session when the retiral of the present Headmaster takes place. The school will be known then simply as Kemnay School, with the status of the former Junior Secondary Schools.

Word has come today also that the Scottish Education Department have sanctioned the further postponement of Miss Jeannie Bremner's retirement until the end of the summer vacation, 1949.

March 25 1948: The School Hot Dinner Scheme inaugurated by the Headmaster soon after he took up duty here ended today. The scheme has gone on all these years and been self supporting, the pupils paying a penny a day and receiving as much soup as they wished. The new canteen is due to open any time now.

The Technical Building is now being got ready.

May 6 1948 Thursday: Miss Grant, County organizer for School Meals, was at school seeing the arrangements made for the opening of the Canteen on Tuesday 11th instant. Miss Mitchell, Parkhill, Kemnay is Head Cook, and her assistants are Mrs Elrick, Cassie Cottage, and Mrs Walker, Tantallon. There are two servers, Mrs Emslie, Atholl Cottage, and Mrs Bell, The Knowe, but the latter is not able to take up duty till a week later as she has to give a week's notice to Hotel, where she is working meantime. Mrs Jack Walker is acting as interim server.

May 17 1948: The number of pupils taking hot dinners this week is 164. The idea has caught on and the scheme promises to be an unqualified success. It means, of course, much extra work, both in the way of supervision, planning the service and the clerical work. Also there are hitches every day which have to be met, either ovens not functioning, a break down in potato peeler, fuses in electricity, and there has to be constant reference to Aberdeen Office. The main thing is the success of the communal school two course midday meal. The supervisors this week are Miss Harper and Mr Gall.

June 28 1948 Monday: Today, two days before the actual closing date, the School Prize Giving was held owing to the Headmaster's intention to attend the Holyrood Garden Party on Wednesday afternoon, 30th instant. The occasion was also the Headmaster's retiral and farewell to the school which he has served for the last twenty five years.

Dealing with the re-grading of the school the Headmaster explained how this change had come about. There was first the general fall in school population which affected the whole country. The simple fact that families were much smaller was patent to everyone. Besides that general cause there was the local fall in school population. Kemnay was becoming a favourite residence for retired people, whose children, if there were any, were all grown up and away from Kemnay. Then there was the plain fact, unpalatable perhaps, but true, that very few of the local pupils continued beyond the third year. Thus in the fourth year this session there was not one pupil from Kemnay village or parish.

The Secondary Department had lost its chief feeder when Alford School was made a full three year language Secondary School. When the present Headmaster took over Kemnay School there were over thirty pupils coming by train from Alford and Upper Donside. Now we were lucky to have six pupils from the upper area in the 4th year. All these factors, operating now over a long period, had induced the Education Committee, in full consultation with the Headmaster, to re-grade the school as a Junior Secondary School. Pupils who wished to go on to a full Leaving Certificate Course would be taken to Inverurie Academy after completing the third year at Kemnay.

Meantime the pupils in 4th and 5th years would be allowed to complete their course at Kemnay School. The changes would affect only the very small number of pupils going further with education. How small that number was was evident when it was stated that one girl of the third year – not a Kemnay girl – was going to Inverurie next year, and one boy, an incomer to the village, was going to Robert Gordon's College, Aberdeen.

Further points in the Headmaster's Report were the success of the Annual Open Air Shakespeare Play, which, in the material way, supplied all the funds that kept the school going, quite apart from the educative value of the performance of the play itself. The prizes, the library, the pictures which were so notable a feature of the school, the sports equipment, the very chairs on which the audience sat, these were only some of the material benefits accruing to the school from the Shakespeare play. Apart from that source the school had very little in way of endowment. There was the Miss Yeats Prize to the Dux of the Primary School, and also her prize to the pupil in the Qualifying Class who made most progress in the year. That fund had been augmented this year on the death of Miss Yeats's brother, by a further gift of £50, invested so as to give the interest for prize-fund. There was the School Dux prize of three guineas, given by Dr. Gordon Davidson, Grimsby, but the likelihood now was that, with the ceasing of the school as a full Secondary School, the prize would lapse. There was diversity of opinion about the giving of prizes. The present Headmaster believed in it and had provided for it by his various activities, as already stated.

Mention was also made of the new Technical Room which was not yet completed, and which would allow the old Benchwork room to be used purely as a classroom in Mathematics and Geography.

The Dining Hall has been hung with pictures representing dinner throughout the ages.

The most notable addition this year to the school equipment has been the provision of amplifier and loud speakers to the various Halls and Rooms at a cost of over £84 by Messrs Alexanders Ltd, Union Street Aberdeen. Portfolios also have been specially made by Taylor's Art Saloon as containers to hold pictures etc., and one has been provided for each classroom or teacher.

All these items have been met from the Activities Fund. The School Magazine, which was founded and edited by the Headmaster, and which ran for three years, 1925-27, has been bound, and copies presented to the County Region Library, the Aberdeen City Library, and Kemnay School Library.

The gross receipts from this year's Shakespeare Play amount to £93 12s 6d.

July 10 1948 Saturday: Mr Burnett, the laird of Kemnay, died late this evening.

July 13 1948 Tuesday: This afternoon the funeral of the laird took place from St Anne's Episcopal Church to the parish kirkyard where the Burnett family is buried.

Mr Burnett has been a good friend of Kemnay School and has always taken the greatest interest in the annual Open Air Shakespeare Play performed in his policies as well as in the general welfare of the community. He was a gentleman of the old school.

July 14 1948: Since the closing of the school the Headmaster has been busy clearing up the accumulated papers and documents of twenty five years.

John A Morgan

One of the more illustrious pupils to pass through the portals of Kemnay School was the late John A. Morgan. Born in the village, the son of a quarry worker, he savoured the joys of music from an early age, his father being fiddler in a local dance band.

John had a natural bent for music and his father gave him all encouragement, teaching him the skills of the violin from a very early age. John received further tuition in Aberdeen.

He left school at fifteen and started work at the Comers shop at Midmar as general do a'thing. Following this introduction to the world of commerce, John taught music in the schools in the Kemnay area. He also played in a local dance band. He was appointed choirmaster at Kemnay Parish Church in 1938, and held this post until he left to serve in the war.

It was while serving with the armed forces that his ability to entertain his fellow man became obvious. Following his war service, entertaining became his way of life. He toured all round the world taking a breath of Scotland to exiles in all corners of the globe. He worked many times on radio and television as well as theatres and music halls throughout the land.

John died in his adopted Devon in 1990, and we print, with the permission of his family his poem entitled 'Return to Kemnay'.

Return to Kemnay

>Noo far awa' frae limelicht's glare,
>Frae thumpin' drum an' trumpets blare,
>I stan' atap the aull stane stair
>>Ahin' Star Hoose:
>Thro' half a cent'ry's years an' mair
>>My min' rins loose.

>The seasons an' the years roll roon'
>An' halcyon days are gone too soon,
>But fine I min' whan jist a loon
>>An' in my prime

Thae steps I lowpet up an' doon
    Twa at a time.

But noo I'm slowin' doon, I doot
Sic exercise wad wear me oot
High livin' an' forbidden fruit
    Hae cramp't my muscles
An' my aull hairt compleens aboot
    My bluid corpuscles!

What memories sweet come back tae me
O' happy days that used tae be
Whan tae the hills I raise my e'e
    This bonnie day
Nae fairer sicht 'twixt Don an' Dee
    Could I survey.

Gin only heav'n wad in me noo
The bardic fire o' Burns renew
Tae set the scene, tae paint the view
    An' sing its praise;
But sic a gift is gi'en tae few
    O's nooadays.

The sun's gien autumn frost a fleg;
Noo Tillyfowrie, Tough, Tambeg,
Aul' Monymusk an' Clett an' Keig
    Lie bathed in licht,
While up the howe ilk hill an' craig
    Stan's clear an' bricht.

Straucht forrit ow'r the Braes o' Mar,
Amang the hielan' hills afar,
I see the tap o' Lochnagar
    Abune Strathdee,
An' tae the west, ahin' Manar,
    Aul' Benachie

Aul' Benachie whaur Gadie rins
Thro' peaty bogs, ow'r rocky linns

Wi' heather, bracken, breem an' whins
      Her banks alang.
(There's nae a Gordon man but kens
      Yon couthy sang.)

I've wandered by the silvery Tweed
An' by the Thames at Runnymede;
I've watched the sparklin' waters speed
      Alang the Spey,
An' tho' they're lovely streams indeed,
      This I maun say:

Clear windin' doon the Alford Vale,
Caressin' mony a hill an' dale,
The bonnie Don can never fail
      Tae charm my e'e:
O' rivers I maun ever hail
      Her 'Queen' tae me!

It's hairst-time noo ow'r a' the lan',
Fulfillin' Nature's annual plan
An' 'combines' thrash on ilka han'
      Whaure'er ye look
Nae mony noo could mak' a ban'
      Or scythe an stook

Spine-rackin' toil like howkin' drains
Or spreadin' muck has left 'The Mains';
Noo that's a' dane at nae great pains
      By big machines
Wi' drivers' cabs in case it rains
      An blauds their jeans.

They ca' that 'progress', I suppose
(Progressin' whaur? – lor' only knows!)
Twad be a shame war' we tae lose
      Ilk' aul' tradition;
E'en porritch, kail an' pizzmeal brose
      That built a nation.

Richt glib the names roll aff my tongue
O beauty spots unkent, unsung,
But kent tae me whan I was young
    An' coortin, quines;
Whaur bluebells grew an' briars hung
    Mang scented pines.

Up Bussie's Road by Sunnyside,
Whaur peezies wheep an' pairtricks hide;
Whaur Jamie Philip used tae bide
    In yesteryear,
Or ow'r Don Brig tae tak' a stride
    'Roon Fetternear

Whan strollin' thro' the Wilderness
Or mony anither shady place,
Wi' Hilda, Betty, Jean or Bess
    Upon my airm,
Wad steal the antrin youthful kiss
    That did nae hairm.

I aften wonder whaur they've gane:
A' scatterit far an' wide, I ween;
Some mairried noo, an' some their lane
    Still warslin' on:
Like me, I guess, they aften min'
    O' days doon Don.

The aul' Free Kirk upo' the hill,
Wi' three-faced clock clear-chiming still
Tae mark the 'oors, for guid or ill,
    That mak' oor days.
Aft hae I heard her rafters thrill
    Wi' heav'nly praise:

The Slater's fruity baritone
An' Pheekie Weir's lugubrious drone
Conjoin't their warldly cares tae moan
    An' beg for Manna,
Or waftet up unto the Throne

       In lood hosanna!

An' ben Back Lane in kirkyard green
Whaur sleep my fowks an' mony a frien',
The Aul' Kirk stan's. There aft alane
      I bass't the choir
While Aul' Rob took the tenor strain
      A half scale higher.

I see the elders steppin' slow,
I hear the aul' hymn's ebb an' flow,
"O, Love that wilt not let me go ___ "
      In sombre key:
It mak's me think o' lang ago
      An' dicht my e'e.

There's mony a learned, letter't chiel
An' mony a glaiket gype as weel,
First learn't tae write at Kemnay skweel
      On slate wi' skylie,
A method that's been on repeal
      This gey lang whilie.

A fyow gaed there intent tae learn
But maist had daily breed tae earn
An' Latin never taucht a bairn
      Tae haud a ploo:
Nae Greek was no't tae ca' a churn
      Or milk a coo!

There discipline was stern an' stric';
They ruled us wi' a muckle stick:
If oot o' turn we daur't tae spik
      Ev'n in a whisper,
Or if we tried a jauk or trick,
      We got a blister!

Altho' it had nae lang effect,
If naething else it taucht respect
A trait that's sairly in neglect

In modern time:
It wad guid-livin' fowk protect
    Frae mony a crime.

Is that the half-five train I hear?
It canna be – the train's nae mair:
It's jist a bairnie on the stair
    That's lost 'is ba'
An' wauken't memories hard tae share
    O' things awa'.

What sichts an' soon's noo come tae min'
Whan thinkin' back on days lang syne:
O' trains gaun up an' doon the line,
    The quarry horn;
O' kirk-bells' slow an' solemn chime
    On Sabbath morn:

The Oakbank Pipers lood an' clear
Quick-marchin' doon thro Fetternear,
A' dress't up in their tartan gear
    On kirk parade,
Wi' a' the village oot tae hear
    Their serenade:

O' picnics in the 'Pleasure Park
Wi dancin' on the boord till dark:
Fleet Mither Dow an' Shokey Clark
    In Jig an' reel;
Hec Cruickie sweatin' at the wark
    A hardy chiel!

The band wad play "Kafoozalum"
An' yarkin' feet like voodoo drum
Wad dance a' worries up the lum
    At crackin' pace,
While Johnnie Webster, fu' o' rum,
    Cried "State yer case!"

On lookin' back it a' seems braw,

But lor', we had hard times an' a',
Whan nor'-east win's blew bleak an' raw
    Thro' drivin' rain,
Or winter brocht great drifts o' snaw
    For weeks on en'.

Thro' dubs an' slush we plyter't on
(We've since seen sotters waur gin yon!)
Weel kennin' it wid a' be gone
    Neest sinny day
An' a' forgotten in the fun
    At Hogmanay.

New Year's Day, key-stane o' the year,
Saw frien's come in frae far an' near
An' glesses clinket fu' o' cheer
    Tae toast each ither,
"Guid health an' plenty graith an' gear
    'Til next we gither."

But noo the air is turnin' chill;
Grey mist is swirlin' on the hill
An', tho' I'd like tae linger still,
    I'll need tae gyang,
But I'll be back wi' richt guid will
    Afore ow'r lang.

I'll tak' the weel-kent road again,
Doon Brucie's Brae an' ben Dub Lane;
Mayhap I'll meet some-ane I ken
    Wi' drooth tae cure
An' in the Burnett Arms we'll spen'
    A social 'oor.

So, fareweel Kemnay, hame sweet hame,
Nae ither place tae me's the same.
As lang's I've breath I'll sing yer fame
    Like mighty organ
An' tae these lines append my name
    Yours Aye, John Morgan.

Acknowledgements

The Kemnay Local History group wish to thank all those who have given help and encouragement in this venture. Many people have unknowingly contributed, and may be surprised to see themselves in print. At the outset, a number of folk were interviewed regarding their schooldays. Typescripts of these interviews have been deposited in the Academy library for use as an archive by the pupils studying History. Sadly some of those interviewed have since died, but it is satisfying that their school memories have been recorded for posterity.

Considerable help has been received from Grampian Regional Archives, staff at Aberdeen University Library, Department of Special Collections and Archives, Aberdeen Central Library, North East Scotland Library Services, and to all those the group are deeply grateful.

Mrs S L Milton allowed free access to the Burnett Archives at Kemnay House which yielded previously unknown details of the old school at Kemnay.

The Community Education Department at Kemnay Academy provided funding for the interviewer, Sheena Cobb, at the start of the project, as well as for photocopies of log and minute books.

The family of the late John A Morgan have given their permission to reproduce his poem and the Aberdeen University Review have allowed us to reprint the appreciations to J Minto Robertson. Mary H Duncan and Gordon R Ingram gave valuable help in writing the chapter on J Minto Robertson.

Thanks to those who donated photographs and to the following who helped to identify characters in them; Jean Pirie, Blanche Morris, Janet Buchan, Isabel M Emslie, Mary H Duncan, Gordon R Ingram, Mr & Mrs Walter Gilbert. It is hoped to deposit the photographs in the Academy library.

Photographic work was carried out by Roger Esson and Stuart Chalmers. Thanks are due to David Duthie for producing drawings of the school, Neil Calder for relettering Andrew Stevenson's gravestone, Miss Ann Clark, Alford, for supplying a school badge in pristine condition and allowing it to be copied and to Philip Jacquet for advice on layout and publication.